Meditation
and
TAROT

©Troy Parkinson

About the Author

Chanda Parkinson's rather eclectic background and passions include the arts and music, professional work in the nonprofit sector, owning and operating several businesses, volunteering as a social justice and human rights advocate, and mothering three children. An early life interest in Christian theological studies expanded to include astrology, tarot, Celtic shamanism, folk magic, and witchcraft, which she continues to devour with great fervor. She has been a student and practitioner of psychic development since the late 1990s. Chanda has been a professional psychic intuitive, tarot reader, astrologist and spiritual teacher since 2006. Her greatest joy is witnessing others discovering and stepping into their own natural spiritual gifts. *Meditation and Tarot* is her second published book.

Meditation *and* TAROT

connect
with the
cards
to
develop your
inner vision

Chanda Parkinson

Llewellyn Publications | Woodbury, Minnesota

FIRST EDITION
First Printing, 2024

Book design by R. Brasington
Cover design by Shira Atakpu
Editing by Laura Kurtz
Heirophant Tarot card cover art by Elisabeth Alba
Interior art by
    Abigail Larson—art from *Dark Wood Tarot*: 93, 104, 119, 134, 138, 146, 165, 169
    Elisabeth Alba—art from *The Everyday Witch Tarot*: 89, 107, 115, 123, 127, 130, 151, 162
    Leeza Robertson—art from *Mermaid Tarot*: 97, 101, 111, 142, 155, 159

Photography is used for illustrative purposes only. The persons depicted may not endorse or represent the book's subject.

Llewellyn Publications is a registered trademark of Llewellyn Worldwide Ltd.

Library of Congress Cataloging-in-Publication Data (Pending)
ISBN: 978-0-7387-7395-7

Llewellyn Worldwide Ltd. does not participate in, endorse, or have any authority or responsibility concerning private business transactions between our authors and the public.
    All mail addressed to the author is forwarded but the publisher cannot, unless specifically instructed by the author, give out an address or phone number.
    Any internet references contained in this work are current at publication time, but the publisher cannot guarantee that a specific location will continue to be maintained. Please refer to the publisher's website for links to authors' websites and other sources.

Llewellyn Publications
A Division of Llewellyn Worldwide Ltd.
2143 Wooddale Drive
Woodbury, MN 55125-2989
www.llewellyn.com

Printed in the United States of America

Other Books by Chanda Parkinson

Finding Your Calm

Meditations for Psychic Development

The Secret Psychic

Dedication

I dedicate this book to those brave souls who have held the tarot torch shining brightly throughout the ages. In deepest gratitude to my beloved mentors Peg Schwandt and Sheri Woxland, who believed in me, and were guiding lights at the beginning of my own tarot journey. May I do your memory and life's work justice through my continued practice and teaching.

Contents

Foreword

For years we tarot lovers have employed tarot for divination, guidance, and self-discovery. Today people use their cards for journaling, creativity, and problem-solving. And let's not forget the cards' original function—playing games. From fortunetelling to fortune creating, tarot seems able to do it all. Since the 1970s, we've explored tarot through a psychological lens, which has proved extremely fruitful. In recent years, we've discovered that tarot is a natural companion for contemplative practices, meditation among them. Fortunately for us, these two practices—tarot and meditation—have been put into a creative cauldron, blended with experience, seasoned with wisdom, and presented here for the benefit of all. Meditating with the cards helps us learn the cards, ourselves, and the world better.

In this book, Chanda Parkinson offers a truly fresh perspective on learning and working with the cards. With kindness and insight, she guides us through experiences that combine the power of tarot and of meditation to deepen mindfulness, cultivate intuition, and unlock our inner wisdom. Meditating with the cards is a unique method of learning about them. The knowledge gained through meditation is a direct experience with the card itself.

Tarot is an organic, evolving expression of wisdom. When we interact with tarot in meditation, we gain something that cannot be gained elsewhere or in any other way. How often can a book promise something that special ... and deliver?

Whether you are new to meditation or tarot—or an experienced practitioner in either—the techniques presented here will inspire you to explore new ways in which tarot can enrich your spiritual journey, with both readings and meditative activities. By aligning your inner self with the archetypes and symbols of tarot in this integrative, active way, you will discover new depths of self-awareness and a greater sense of connection to the universe, and, of course, to the cards.

Chanda's approach is accessible, practical, and relatable with clear guidance for each meditation. In addition to all the necessary meditation- and tarot-related basics, this book also includes other activities—such as how to strengthen your relationship with your deck—which are useful to the beginner and seasoned reader alike. We all know that getting the right answer means asking the right question, and Chanda helps us hone this skill as well. All these elements make *Meditation and Tarot* a valuable resource for anyone interested in using tarot as a tool for personal growth or for anyone seeking unique experiences with their cards.

Get ready to deepen your meditation practice and unlock the transformative power of the tarot. This is serious and important work, indeed, but let us remember that tarot began life as a game. Playfulness is part of tarot's DNA for a reason. All work and no play make for a sad, weary spiritual seeker. Expect to have fun along with the revelations. What a journey you are about to begin!

—Barbara Moore

Introduction

There exists a magical space of exploration when spiritual practices such as meditation and psychic tools such as tarot merge to the enhanced benefit of the practitioner. It is through this spirit of exploration that we can crack open a greater capacity for depth and meaning in our lives. Blending mystical tools and practices combined with enhanced skill is the true path of the Magician! What a rich pathway that is available to us all.

Meditation is a time-honored practice of calming the mind that lets us feel into our life with clarity. It promotes mental peace and creates a receptive and open space for receiving insights. It reduces stress levels, helps balance the nervous system, and creates a blank canvas on which we create our inner vision.

Tarot cards open us up to a metaphoric world within. Tarot is a psychological and divinatory tool; it guides us to understanding our inner world, behaviors, thoughts, emotions, and choices and helps us realize potential outcomes to life events. Tarot cards alone do nothing without the active engagement and conscious attention of the reader. The cards themselves are pieces of guidance waiting for us to uncover from our intuitive memory. They can point the arrow directly at the problem and offer possible solutions.

When I'm reading tarot cards for someone in a mental jam, I can feel the visceral release of that energy and jam through emotion with a subsequent freeing of the mind. It sometimes feels like the moment before a baby is born, just at the quickening. The revelations in the cards combined with the calming forces of meditation relieve the pressure those moments birth into reality. In freeing the mind, there is a greater potential to shift the thought process or even a possible course of action, as different scenarios become available. Tarot can alleviate the pressure of the birthing process to bring in new, fresh perspectives. When we remain in our heads still trying to logically sort out a mental jam, we further disconnect from the wisdom receptors in our bodies, which include our five senses and our sixth sense. Our bodies reveal more of the story to us when also engaged in the process. Meditation can serve as the body's method of relaxing into a more receptive mode. When our intuition is at the ready, our natural receiving mechanisms ignite offering insights and solutions. We are resourcing our multi-sensory organism and this can lend a powerful and grounded approach for life guidance.

You don't need to be a visual person to enjoy the benefits of a meditative tarot practice. Meditation slows down the body's biorhythms, putting us in a steady mode for psychic receiving. We all receive psychic information differently because our individual hardwiring is not the same. That hardwiring includes a combination of our internal compass known as our intuition, our third eye activation, our multi-sensory capabilities including our sixth sense, and sensitivities to psychic stimuli. If you are built to feel rather than to receive through visions, your relationship with tarot will unfold through feelings, emotion, intuition, and imagination.

Meditation with the tarot is the way to discover their deeper meanings without the added pressure of sifting and sorting through books and online resources. Removing the information overload will bring you closer to them. In this way, meditation and tarot are highly compatible. Both tools lend the power to visualize, sense, or feel through the quiet spaces of our minds and hearts to reveal important insights. Tarot links us to a greater field of information than meditation alone, and meditation clarifies the meanings of the tarot. They are incredibly compatible practices. During a Tarot Meditation, your consciousness will be opened to the infinite possibilities of each card. You will be guided by your inner wisdom to see things in the cards that you've never seen before. You will be open to unique personal experiences sparked by the characters featured on the cards. And when you've made this soulful connection with each character, their wisdom will be more accessible.

You do not need any prior experience with tarot cards or meditation to learn and benefit from this book. It's also perfectly acceptable to keep your rituals simple; lighting a candle and sitting down to shuffle is sufficient. Nothing more complex is needed. Adding crystals and stones or lighting incense or herbs for smoke clearing are ways to expand an already existing practice.

This book centers a beginners approach to reading tarot, including how to think about the cards, different ways to work with them, understanding how the deck is organized, how to meditate and journal with them, make them personal, and use them practically in your life. Some tarot practitioners insist that you read both upright and reversed (that is, when you have drawn the cards that are upside down) interpretations. Reading reversals is a more advanced tarot technique, so we will stick with upright meanings only. My approach has always been drawing cards I am meant to see at that particular moment.

The two things tarot and meditation have in common are that both are tools you can practice and improve over time. Formatting a meditative tarot practice isn't complicated. Once you've handled logistics such as where to meditate, what sort of meditation to use, and what cards to work with and how, we will have you well on your way to a successful practice. This book is designed to calm any fears you may have about your ability to learn and use tarot. You absolutely can do this.

When you know the reasons why you are interested in incorporating tarot into your daily life, you will be able to create a tarot practice that is fulfilling and supportive. Tarot cards become like a good bestie and counselor, helping you get out of your own way, showing you the truth inside your head and your heart, giving you perspective, and yes, sometimes revealing things you aren't necessarily ready to hear. If nothing else, tarot is honest. It can sink you deeper into your psyche to learn more about what makes you tick and release the clutter in your mind to more clearly see your way forward.

I bought my first deck of tarot cards in 2003, when I was pregnant with my first child. I remember the day distinctly: intense feelings of excitement about what was in store and what sort of learning journey I was about to begin simultaneously overwhelmed me. As I opened the pack and began shuffling the cards, I had a strange sense of familiarity. It was an odd yet comfortable feeling, like meeting up with a long lost friend.

There is no doubt I was intimidated about beginning the road to understanding tarot. However, always a perpetual and avid spiritual learner, I chose to embrace the unknown and surrender. It took time, patience, and plenty of experimentation before I realized the journey to becoming a tarot reader was best approached with one part learning and one part reflection. Devoting hours to memorizing meanings of the cards simply wasn't going to work. The more I tried to remember what the card meant, the less I could call upon the meaning in my mind during tarot readings. I knew I needed to change something, so I set aside the piles of tarot books and instead centered myself in the feelings, thoughts, intuitive impressions, and imagery the cards invoked. It was a true moment of liberation, as if someone opened a window of a hot room and the cool breeze blew in. Letting go of trying to memorize meanings or how to perfectly interpret the cards felt good.

To strip away the complication of the tarot, I developed a technique of studying and meditating with the cards I still use to this day. This book is the culmination of years of practice. I hope you find a path forward that is simple to use, and effective. I have been teaching tarot classes for more than fifteen years. The stories and reasons people embark on a tarot journey are intricately varied and unique to their own path. What I observed over time was a common surfacing theme: people want to discover a way to use the tarot that simplifies the process and a method for knowing the cards without having to memorize their meanings. If you are searching for an approach that doesn't have you on the endless study train, it's here—you are holding it. Tarot reading is intricate and complex, but it's also fun. I am going to offer a way to develop a rich, deep relationship with the tarot through the use of meditation.

This book begins with the basics of meditation and tarot. If you've never meditated or picked up a tarot deck before, by the end of that chapter you will know thoroughly how to do both of those things, how to begin using them, and how they fit together. I offer plenty of options, examples, and ideas for developing a successful meditation routine as well as plenty of tips and guidance in choosing a tarot deck and how to begin studying them. You are not required to be an expert to begin this journey.

Next, we will explore in depth the portion of the tarot deck known as the twenty-two major arcana. We will explore the ways in which each of those cards represents the various characteristics of our personalities, pivotal moments on our life paths, and aspects of our psyche. After that, I offer the planetary and zodiac ruler of each card; establish a working meaning, a meditation, an affirmation or prayer, and a journal prompt you can use with each.

After the major arcana, we will explore the breakdown of the minor arcana, otherwise known as the suits of the tarot deck, their associated elements, the comparisons/contrasts in the suits, the meaning of the numbers on the cards, a brief interpretation, and a meditation exercise and journal prompt for each suit. In addition, we will discover the court cards' personality traits and characteristics—they are rich, complex characters who fill in the spaces of our life story. We will get to know who they are in our own lives, which will assist in identifying their personalities when we use them.

Little did I know the day I bought my first tarot deck that I would eventually become a reader and teacher. To this day, it is the tool I use the most frequent for myself and others. I hope this book provides a method you can quickly use to get started or deepen an already thriving practice. Whatever your journey, your own tarot story, your reasons and methods, this book will add an edge of mystery, revealing your deepest secrets and helping you find your way.

When you are ready to expand beyond a more basic understanding of the tarot, I would encourage you add other books to your library. Here are a few of my favorites that will definitely add to this knowledge and take you beyond the basics. *Tarot for Real Life* by Jack Chanek, *The Ultimate Guide to the Rider Waite Tarot* by Johannes Fiebig and Evelin Burger, *Llewellyn's Little Book of Tarot* by Barbara Moore, and *The Fearless Tarot* by Elliot Adam.

I chose three tarot decks to highlight in the major arcana section of this book.

I find the world of mermaids and the magic of the sea enchanting, which is so beautifully portrayed by images in the *Mermaid Tarot*. Creators Leeza Robertson and Julie Dillon so masterfully present a whimsical yet spiritually stirring representation of the universal tarot themes and fascinating mermaid mythology. I knew these images would appeal to empathic and intuitively proficient readers.

The *Dark Wood Tarot* by Sasha Graham and Abigail Larson came to me as a surprise gift. Once I opened the beautiful packaging with deck and book, I was so taken by the depth and emotional interpretation of the universal themes in the traditional tarot I knew it would be the perfect deck to include for several of my favorite major arcana cards such as Strength and the Hanged Man. The images in this deck speak to those who are unafraid of facing their own inner intensity and shadow side.

I also knew I wanted a deck to convey more modern day scenes and people. The *Everyday Witch Tarot* by Deborah Blake and Elisabeth Alba instantly sparked my curiosity. As a witch myself, I found the playful colors, clothing, symbols, familiars, and the centering of witchy scenes to be not only comforting but also quirky and creative depictions of the variety of ways in which we work our craft. This deck definitely put me under its spell, and I'm so proud to include it here!

CHAPTER ONE

Meditation Basics

Meditation is a time-honored method for calming the mind. The link between quieting the mind and the positive effects on physical and mental health are undeniable. In addition, there have been correlations made between meditation and increased creativity, spontaneous flashes of insight, enhanced problem solving, and improved relationships. Our modern lifestyles can have a chaotic and scattered energy. Time spent in a dedicated meditation prac tice lifts the burden of that intensity and prepares us to deal with our lives more effectively.

In the psychic arts, we also use meditation to activate our third eye, the area on our body located near the pineal gland. When activated, this area of the body behaves as a gateway to connect us to information, data, and messages in the expanse of feelings and data residing in the subtle energy field. It can connect us with other mystical realms to increase activity in our dreams, achieve astral travel (an out of body experience), and connect with loved ones who have crossed over. When our third eye is activated, our sixth sense, or our psychic antennae is heightened. This creates the optimal environment for receiving.

Meditation Methods

There is no right or wrong way to meditate. I am uncomfortable sitting for long periods of time in silence. Although highly effective for some, that form of meditation isn't the best for me. I personally do best with a guided visualization, sound healing with drums or crystal bowls, breathing meditations, or walking in the woods. If you've never meditated before, just embrace that it may take some time before you grow comfortable with what it looks like for yourself. The following are some excellent ways in which to engage your third eye through meditation.

Candle Gazing

Candle gazing can be a wonderful and comforting way to meditate. Light a candle, sit in a dimly lit or dark room, turn on some soft soothing music and watch the candle flame dance. Observe the flame like there is nothing else in the room and fixate your gaze while softening your breath. Notice how the candle flame dances in response to merging with your own energy field.

Breathing

Breathing techniques are an excellent ways to meditate. Breath is a powerful life giving force of energy that puts your body naturally in a calmer state. It just requires a little focus and a plan. My first favorite breath technique is alternate nostril breathing (also known as *nadī shodhana*). Take in air through your nose by plugging one nostril and inhaling, hold in the air, plug the opposite nostril, and blow the air out. Then take in air, hold it, plug the opposite nostril, blow the air out, and repeat. It will definitely empty your mind and get you in the right headspace for meditation. Try it ten times, and notice how instantly calm and centered you feel. The benefits of alternate nostril breathing include nervous system balance, minimizing the stress response, lowering blood pressure, and promoting a feeling of balance. My other favorite technique is just a simple breath in through your nose and out through your mouth for several repetitions. Five to ten minutes of breathing puts you in a receptive, calm, and open state of mind and can increase energy.

Movement

Whenever you move your body through dance, jumping on a trampoline, yoga, tai chi, walking, stretching, swimming, running, or climbing, you are centering your mind around a task for a period of time, which can be incredibly meditative. Have you noticed when you are doing something like that how difficult it is to think about anything else? I love moving meditations and use them frequently in my own life. I still like to climb trees! The combination of movement and breathing can bring about an incredible release of pent up physical energy while simultaneously releasing mental clutter.

Nature

You don't need to be an outdoor enthusiast to incorporate nature into your meditation routines. Whether you occupy an urban dwelling, a suburban bungalow, a cabin in the woods, or a sprawling country home, finding a space that includes trees or plants, dirt, open space, and sky is a wonderful way to feel a sense of one with everything around you. If you are urban, check out local parks and public building grounds. Often they have gardens as part of their landscape, and most of the time they are open to the public. A city zoo, conservatory, or botanical garden is excellent. It doesn't even have to be your own home. Something as simple as placing a small herb garden on a building rooftop with a folding chair while you bathe in the sunlight, can bring just the lift in your mood and set the tone for receiving messages.

Chores

Household chores are an excellent meditative activity. While not always the most fulfilling method, some days it has to do for busy working parents like me. Knowing I have a sink full of dishes to methodically tend to at the end of the day with warm water on my hands allows me to breathe and reflect. I imagine washing away the concerns and worries of the day down the drain. It is soothing and centering. Vacuuming is also a great way to change the energy in a room. If things are feeling funky energetically, try it! You'll be amazed to notice how removing dust and dirt cleanses and clears a space. And it's rigorous exercise.

Your Relaxation Your Way

Meditation need not be a silent, still affair devoid of sensory stimulation. For example, I love getting out my essential oils diffuser, putting in some lavender, lighting a candle, putting a hot water bottle on my feet or chest, covering up with a weighted blanket, and putting on noise-canceling headphones. I typically stay in that zone for only twenty minutes, since being still is not the most comfortable for me. What I've found is that the right music streaming through my headphones can instantly lift the heaviness from my day. I emerge a lighter version of myself, one of my single most important goals for establishing a mediation routine I love, and that works for me.

Be curious about how you prefer to relax. A combination of understanding your own temperament and attention span can greatly assist in selecting the best meditation routine. Use these probing questions to further understand your own preferred rhythms, attention span, and other personal needs before beginning. It is important to manage expectations for this process. Knowing yourself and your habits helps establish a routine that is successful.

Time and Approach

How much time can you commit each week to meditation? Remember, meditation doesn't need to be lengthy to be effective—just ten to fifteen minutes a day or a few times a week is plenty. Do you feel like you can discipline yourself to meditate? I believe consistency in a meditation is key to its power to heal and keep our vessel open. A goal of three times a week is a great start, increasing the frequency as you go. Do you have an easy or difficult time sitting still and being quiet? Being honest with yourself about this will make all the difference.

Environment and Sounds

Do you prefer a dark or well-lit environment when you relax? This detail can make a huge difference in how deep you'll go into your meditation. Don't do something that isn't comfortable. Are you open to using technology for your meditation? There's a plethora of device applications and YouTube tracks that can easily and readily support any meditation. I love shamanic practitioner Sandra Ingermann's drumming tracks and visualizations on YouTube. Steven Halpern's crystal bowl sound healing tracks are subtle, soothing, and gorgeous. I also have a singing bowl in my home office that I use to set the frequency and lift the vibration in my room before I meet with clients. I use the Moonly app on my phone, which offers daily tips on the phases of the moon, as well as a guided meditation I find both super grounding and supportive. I would invite you to research and explore all the possibilities, and experiment until you find ones that you love.

Music

Good music that brings you joy and reaches your soul raises your vibrational frequency. It doesn't have to be spiritual or meditation music. Can you easily set aside time where you know you won't be interrupted? As a busy mom of three, this is particularly challenging for me, but I set up activities for my kids and make sure they know not to come in my room when the door is closed. When you are in a meditative state, disruptions can be jarring, so it's best to come back slowly from those blissful spaces.

Create a Meditation Routine

Here you'll find suggestions for creating a successful meditation routine. Set reasonable expectations based on your schedule and lifestyle. Avoid bedtime, so you know you will be able to stay awake. If you are new to meditation, consider beginning with five minutes a day, and increase incrementally each week by five more minutes. You'll know when you have reached a comfortable timing for you. Some need shorter and some need longer timeframes, depending on temperament and concentration levels. All time amounts are perfect. Try out different locations. Do you prefer a dark or brightly lit room? All rooms have a vibe. Try every one to see which is going to be a better fit. Determine what you need to be comfortable. Tell others in your home you are beginning a meditation routine. Remind them before you begin your meditation you need privacy. Invite their quiet, care, and support. Have something handy to record what you experienced during meditation such as a journal or voice memo. Sometimes visual images will appear, and you could experience feelings, colors, messages, or other spontaneous phenomena. You'll want to keep track of whatever you experienced for later review.

CHAPTER TWO

Tarot Basics

The tarot is a living and breathing, ever-changing yet consistent storytelling tool for our lives. The qualities and characteristics displayed on the faces of the cards come to life as real life characters we encounter on a daily basis in our lives, our families, our neighborhoods, our jobs, the world, and they also represent us. They reveal our milestones, add shape to chaotic days, and bring focus and clarity to otherwise confusing moments. Furthermore, tarot reveals patterns of behavior and cycles we all go through in our lives. We all have moments in our lives that include new beginnings, birthing ideas, making changes, making decisions, turmoil, endings, undergoing a crisis, grief, loss, guilt, joy, excitement, and all the while doing the best we can. The stories in the tarot represent the human condition. They show us at any given moment the aspects of our psyche and we are living out. They show us our own life stories playing out before our eyes.

Tarot is a mystical tool. While it holds an element of mystery, it is certainly not—as some would have us believe—something that opens us to evil forces. If you heard in your own religious upbringing that tarot or divinatory card use is heretical or against the will of God, you may feel hesitant or even fearful. De-stigmatizing the tarot happens when we understand more clearly its uses and welcome it as a resourceful friend into our daily lives.

In my first exposure to a tarot deck, I felt secretly anxious about them but tried not to divulge my trepidation. Like most people, my only previous exposure to tarot came through movies and television. A fortuneteller dressed in long flowing clothing, behaving mysteriously, sitting in a dark room with a crystal ball while laying cards on the table was the only image clouding my mind. Opening myself up to the idea of someone doing a tarot card reading was definitely beyond my comfort zone, but there was enough curiosity to quiet the fear. It was fascinating to hear someone else who could not have possibly known certain things about me so accurately describe events, circumstances, even feelings I was having at the moment about my life. It was so moving that I immediately drove to a bookstore to purchase my own deck. Fascination swiftly turned to serious study, and I searched for mentors who could enlighten me on the workings of the cards and how to construct proper tarot readings for others and myself. I have been reading cards ever since.

Opening a tarot deck for the first time sparks a cosmic wrestling match within. When your curiosity is strong and your intentions are clear, the realm of exploration held within this bountiful storytelling tool will amaze and astonish you. You suddenly find yourself in the midst of a series of visual images that cast upon your life like a mirror and behave like a magnifying glass to your heart, bringing to your conscious mind thoughts, feelings, suppressed longings, and direct guidance.

Many times over the span of years I have worked with tarot, I have personally sat pondering a card or a series of cards but simply drew a blank. After meditating, breathing, holding steady with my gaze casting over the cards and images, suddenly a major *a-ha!*

moment of awareness hit me like an ocean wave. We can remove the need to make this practice merely a technical left-brained process. It is nice to have a format to work within, but if we can also add in periodic doses of patience and wait for the images to inspire a message or bit of guidance, it's worth the wait.

Part of reading tarot includes disciplined effort and not allowing periodic ambivalence about the card meanings themselves to throw us off course. Just like building any relationship, getting to know tarot through a welcoming attitude of curiosity will enhance your practice greatly.

In our ever-evolving life, sometimes things need to be left to work themselves out, while other situations involve a more direct series of action steps. Tarot cards can assist in strategizing the plan of action, and assist us in re-orientating our minds about a problem. When our emotions cloud a situation we are going through, tarot has the added benefit of clearing the mental cloudiness and confusion by showing us what we may not have seen before.

Purposes

Before beginning your own meditative tarot journey, it is worth considering the various purposes of the cards. I believe having a clear intention is the basis for any successful psychic tool use, especially tarot. As this tool has great power to align you with profound revelations and appropriate guidance, you want to be crystal clear why you are interested in the study and practice of the tarot.

There are many reasons why people choose to work with this potent and clarifying helper. Framing your tarot practice is the first step. Learning about the cards themselves, how they work, interpretations, and tarot spreads are secondary. You may find yourself in more than one category on this list, and that's absolutely perfect. You may choose to grant yourself the permission to explore and try out all of the reasons, until you better understand what the best fit is for your own tarot practice.

Everyone has different goals and needs for using psychic tools such as tarot and meditation. Allow these examples to assist you in discovering a framework and motivation for your own practice. Your motivations may change for using the cards as your life evolves and changes. Note that tarot is not a replacement for psychotherapy, especially when suffering from mental illness, severe anxiety, or depression. It is a beneficial supplemental tool when used in an appropriate context and in a conscious, careful, and consistent way. If you suffer from mental illness and are curious whether or not you are ready to use a psychological tool such as the tarot, you can always ask your therapist or psychiatrist.

Problem-Solving

When in a mental jam around a life situation, tarot can adequately and accurately provide you options for how to solve any problem. Actually, all sorts of whimsical and creative information is accessible through tarot's stories and images. With the right question framing, the cards can pinpoint the root of the problem and advise you on how to best move through it.

Divination

Tarot is a tool for divination, which is the practice of determining the hidden significance or causes of events. In addition, it can foretell potential outcomes and scenarios. Since our future is not set in stone, and we have the power of free will, I believe it is truly challenging to know the definitive outcome of the questions we ask. However, we can detect future potential, based on things staying the same in the current moment. I generally advise waiting to use cards for future telling until you have a solid grasp on the tarot.

Decision-Making

Whether or not you consider yourself an indecisive person, we all have those moments where it is difficult to decide between the available options. Tarot reveals and releases the mental blocks around the decision itself and can present the option that most strongly matches your own highest good.

Understanding Yourself

Because tarot is also a psychological tool, it represents universal patterns of behavior and human characteristics we all share, making it an invaluable tool for self-awareness. There are times when we are uncertain about why we are behaving, feeling, or thinking a certain way about something. Tarot can help us dig deeper to get at the root of our own personality and behavior. There is tremendous power in realizing the crux of an issue and pivoting to align with our own value systems.

Understanding Others

Just as we can apply the tarot to understanding ourselves, we can also understand the actions and behaviors of others who are in our inner sphere. Seeking understanding through the stories tarot cards provide can assist you in shifting your reactions and communication patterns to improve your relationships. I find tarot brings me much more empathy and compassion for the struggles others face.

Mental Health

Tarot can assist in restoring psychological health by exploring the meaning through the life experiences we are having. Sometimes it can be difficult to see beyond a current obstacle or upsetting situation. Evaluating things from a more objective point of view can assure us that although we may be going through something challenging, those events tend to have an ending. Getting out of the weeds of the mind and into a more positive framework about the circumstances lends mental balance.

In addition to psychological balance, tarot can also provide us emotional balance. There is no arguing that emotional discomfort disrupts our lives; emotional pain is unsettling and destabilizing. Leaning into tarot during moments of emotional discomfort can ease mild anxiety and provide necessary reassurance to come back to center. Incorporating a meditation with tarot practice is incrementally more calming. Over time, you may discover that regular use of meditation and tarot brings overall emotional harmony.

Creativity

You can use tarot cards as a muse. Creative blocks happen, and when you need something visual to inspire you, tarot can help you free your mind. With just the right image, colors, words, or symbols, you can be on your way to the next great idea. I love using tarot to help me write. I whisper to my mind and the supportive forces beyond where I am stuck, then shuffle and draw a few cards, and usually the cards drawn spark a new word, concept, or phrase. Visual artists can benefit from drawing tarot to unlock new layers of creative flow. Organizations, businesses, boards, and project teams can gain insight from mulling over a tarot story together, inducing solutions and new ways of approaching a problem.

Organizing Your Thoughts

If you are notorious for periodic mental traffic jams, join the club. There are times in our lives when we are hit with thinking overload. It's unhealthy to allow the perpetual spin, especially if it's toxic. You can use tarot cards to sort out each individual thought stream. Compartmentalizing different areas of thought can ease the clutter and calm the chaos. Look at each thought one at a time through the lens of tarot. It's not a bad thing to think a lot, however sometimes we need a little help organizing our thoughts so we can feel less controlled by them.

Spirit Communication

Tarot may be used to communicate with spirit guides and loved ones—one of my favorite ways to use it. Although I am a medium, I don't connect as easily with my own loved ones as I do for others. I bypass this obstacle by inviting their presence and conversation through tarot cards. I can pose questions, find out how they are, and ask if there's anything they would like me to know. Obviously it's not the same as having their actual physical presence, yet it's still comforting. You can also use cards to connect with spirit guide wisdom and guidance. Clarify whom you are asking for before you shuffle the cards and you're set. What may seem like a disjointed or confusing effort at first can grow into lovely moments of connection and healing. Don't get discouraged if your efforts take some time to build intimacy with spirit connections.

The Tarot Deck

Learning to read the tarot can be daunting at first but doesn't need to be. Understanding how a tarot deck is organized is simple; once learned, this knowledge gives readers tremendous power over the deck. However, the various ways in which we can interpret each card is multi-faceted depending on where it appears in a tarot spread and on the question originally asked. It is best to first learn how the tarot deck is organized, then discover the patterns between the cards, and finally learn about the individual meanings of the cards. Inundating yourself with the meanings and interpretations scatters your mental energy, causing you to lose focus on the original intent. Card decks of all kinds are built to connect us with our inner worlds, so it is helpful to approach your study methodically with patterns first.

The Major Arcana

A traditional tarot deck consists of seventy-eight cards. Beginning with the Fool and ending with the World, twenty-two of them are known as the major arcana, or "big secret." When drawn, the major arcana carry additional weight in a reading and often become its focal point. These cards often reveal significant turning points, or aspects of our psyche that are currently playing a role. Drawing one or more of those twenty-two cards intensifies the importance of the situation in question, making them worth paying extra attention to. While they appear to be overdramatized versions of real life, they are potent in their application.

Drawing the Death card in a career-related question might be about more than simply solving a work-related dilemma; it may mean the intentional ending of a job or existing or impending job loss. When drawing the Fool or the Chariot, we are aware of the urgency around making a change, or starting something new. The major arcana can have the purifying effect of parsing out the most critical components of any dilemma and presenting them to us in a way that is difficult to deny or ignore. I cannot state how many times I have drawn the Lovers in a tarot reading for someone facing buried relationship trauma, evaluating a current relationship, experiencing a positive surge of happiness in a current relationship, or considering a leap into the dating pool. The cards powerfully reveal deep truths, even if those truths aren't something we wish to evaluate in the moment. I often tell my students to consider whether or not they really want to be shown honest answers to what they are asking before doing so.

The Minor Arcana

The minor arcana or "little secret" includes four suits (Pentacles, Wands, Swords, and Cups) each numbered 1 through 10 in addition to court cards (Page, Knight, Queen, and King). The symbolic imagery, names, along with the number associations of each card evoke certain meanings depending on the placements. I like to think of the minor arcana as being the cards for solving the day-to-day challenges and conundrums in our lives, which are changeable and highly unpredictable. Learning the minor arcana is best by rote memorization of the suits, the element associated with each, and the symbolism behind the numbers of the cards. You can draw aces in different suits. However, if you've drawn a wand (ruled by the fire element, representing our capacity to take action), it will have an entirely different connotation than a cup (ruled by the water element, representing emotion, imagination, and intuition). I often see the minor arcana cards showing up in readings to reveal the beginning, middle, and ending of an issue, that is generally in the present or near future. In addition, they can be helpful guides regarding what is needed to move beyond an obstacle. They are highly changeable, so if you've laid mainly major arcana cards in a reading, it is wise to follow up on that question again soon to see what has changed, if anything.

The Court Cards

These cards represent the qualities and characteristics of our best friends, our parents, colleagues, bosses, lovers, children, neighbors, and community leaders. They are great fun to engage with. To work with the court cards means accepting that when they show up in a reading, it signifies someone else impacting the situation in question. An easy way to absorb the meanings of the court cards is to match them with someone in your life who has a similar quality or essence. For example, I know that if I draw the King of Wands, it rarely represents me and is more likely to resemble someone with the qualities and characteristics similar to my husband, Troy, who embodies the characteristics of this card: ambitious, active, social, warm, funny, and always moving (unless he's sleeping). If I draw the Knight of Swords, it brings to mind my middle child, who is a thinker. She is all about the reasons and arguments, and doesn't mind sharing her own opinions. There is very little that escapes her, and she has an incredibly sharp mind … and tongue. We will explore the court cards more in the second section of this book. Be ready to find the court card that represents you—you may even discover more than one!

Tarot as a Tool

Tarot can be used as a sacred tool for our soul's growth and evolution. The cards drawn during a tarot reading can help provide insight on a challenging problem you've been ruminating over, or uncover and heal difficult emotions you've been processing. Use it to shed light on life decisions. It helps you understand yourself more deeply.

What makes tarot so potent is not that the cards harbor some mystical power or magic per se, it's that they illuminate humankind's most innate dilemmas and desires. That's why we're still using the tarot more than six hundred years after it originated, because humans continue to struggle with the same fundamental emotions and issues. We all want to love and be loved, to feel safe, to be heard. The tarot serves as a tool to tap into these core human emotions and needs.

The word *psychic* is Greek in origin and means "of the soul," prompting the question: what are we really connecting with when we read this popular psychic tool? The cards are embedded with esoteric (spiritual) wisdom. They embody universal themes we all endure. They reveal core parts of ourselves. They present a mirror image of what may be going on in our emotional and psychological landscape at any given moment. The mystical and mysterious part is how the cards are drawn so accurately to reveal what we need to see. Building your own relationship with the tarot offers a tremendous window into your own soul. Leaping off the tarot cliff tests your capacity to trust that the cards will provide this mirror to your soul or at the least tell you where you may be off center in your approach to certain areas of life.

Tarot is also a healing tool. Posing the right questions of the tarot can pierce the fog and bring about penetrating insights that are capable of shifting our own current perspectives. This can generate tremendous mental release and peace. Tarot is organized in such a way to reveal the patterns and cycles we all go through in the human condition. I lean heavily into the tarot to bring calm to my mind, reflect, and understand my own inner workings. Knowing I can also personally plug in to the wisdom contained in the collective consciousness creates a profound sense of order and a thread of continuity throughout daily life I have grown to respect and appreciate.

The symbols embedded throughout the tarot deck are multi-faceted and add a tremendous amount of meaning to the cards. I don't encourage beginning tarot readers to submerse themselves in the myriad of symbols and their meanings; that can come much later. It is enough to discover and play with tarot and authentically build a relationship with the cards and stories. When you are an intermediate and advanced tarot enthusiast, going more in depth with symbols will enrich your readings. However, there are common thematic symbols it is worth mentioning, as they will come up during the meditation exercises in this book. Use this symbol key as a guide through the meditation process, and to support your further learning.

Key of Common Tarot Card Symbols

Gardens: Symbolize the cycle of life, fertility, new growth, nourishment, and spiritual maturity. In some instances they appear to be places where we receive pleasure and respite.

Water: Emotions, compassion, sensitivity, intuition, and imagination. Fluidity represents the need to adapt and adjust depending on the circumstances in question.

Infinity symbol: There is an infinite capacity in humans to begin again, and forever open the door to the processes of transformation.

Double-ended wands: Characterizes those beings in the tarot who act as a conduit between the earthly and spiritual realms. It is more commonly represented by the saying "as above, so below."

Animals: Birds, fish, reptiles, dogs, snakes, horses, and mythical creatures grace the pictures of the tarot. They all have individual and intricate meanings and can be seen as mystical allies of tremendous spiritual support.

Clouds: These important sky movers represent change, ideas, and revelations.

Fruit: Grapes and pomegranates in particular make occasional special appearances. These symbolize prosperity, esoteric wisdom, and showcase the "fruits" of our labor.

Red: There are multiple appearances of this color, and it increases the vitality and passion in those particular cards. Confidence, action, aggression, radiance, willpower, and raw energy are ways to think about this intense color throughout the tarot.

Stars: Cosmic, astrological, or mystical forces involved in the life situation in question.

Winged creatures: Stability amid movement and change. The ability to "lift" or elevate above a difficult situation.

Naked figures: Nudity in tarot removes any barriers from receiving and knowing the truth about a situation. There is tremendous innocence and renewal.

Crowns: Depending on where it shows up, it showcases where we are exuding and embodying leadership and authority in our lives.

Sun: Where there is sunlight shining through the clouds in the tarot, there is another chance, a new dawn, and an opportunity to begin again.

Moon: Depending on the card, the moon can point to repressed emotions, desires, and subconscious fears. It can also signify femininity and working through the shadow side of ourselves.

Minor Arcana Suits, Elements, Number Meanings

I liken the minor arcana to the plot lines of a story that connect the beginning, middle, climax, denouement, and ending. They are the connectors that provide the intricate, more nuanced aspects of what we are going through. They can also show us where we are on the current path of a certain issue or problem—that is, how close we are to the beginning, middle, or ending.

The number sequences are the same for each suit, ace through 10. Studying the suits' card patterns demystifies this portion of the tarot deck and assists the reader in gaining power over the cards themselves. While each card certainly has its own particular meaning, there is a great deal to be gained by studying the patterns and memorizing this brief list of minor arcana symbols.

Suit	Element	Meaning
Wands	Fire	Action, willpower, change, passion, energy, vitality
Swords	Air	Knowledge, communication, power, decisions, thinking
Cups	Water	Receptivity, intuition, imagination, emotion, heart
Pentacles	Earth	Values, stability, money, prosperity, worth, sensuality

Numbers	Meaning
Ace	Potential, opportunity, change, beginning
Two	Partnership, duality, choices, harmony, opposites
Three	Collaboration, help, growth, groups
Four	Effort, rest, reflection, disappointment, pause
Five	Struggle, conflict, change, instability, difficulty
Six	Perseverance, action, realignment, reconciliation
Seven	Control, lessons, endurance, wisdom
Eight	Mastery, achievement, fortune, advancement
Nine	Completion, attainment, transition
Ten	Ending, culmination, arrival, destination

Court Cards

The court cards can often represent characters in the story of your life. They pop up in tarot readings at times when there is another person in your life who is influencing the situation. They can also represent qualities you are being nudged to harness in your own life. Getting acquainted with the characteristics of each member of the court will give you and instant clue regarding who the person is influencing the question at hand, or what characteristics and qualities you are being advised to access. A strong hint can be those in closest proximity to you, i.e. your spouse, children, parents, coworkers, or neighbors.

Here is a simple breakdown of the court card symbolism:

Court Card	Meaning
Page	Young, energetic people, children, free spirit, artistic, innocent
Knight	Young adult, impulsive, ruthless, reckless, strong, stubborn
Queen	Feminine, receptive, leadership, nurturing, wisdom, composure
King	Masculine, decisive, active, leadership, detachment, maturity

You now have a foundational basis for the layout of the tarot deck and some of the more common symbols and patterns highlighted. Knowing this and thinking about the similarities between something you may already be familiar with and the tarot deck is a great first step to navigating the deck. Life has cycles and patterns. Studying the patterns and cycles present throughout the tarot further reduces it to a simple and practical tool. There is a tremendous amount of complexity to the tarot. Parsing out the separate pieces of the tarot brings a systematic manageable format for learning.

CHAPTER THREE

Preparing to Meditate with the Tarot

So now you've found the best space for your tarot and meditation practice. Embracing this is not an exact science, but always a work in progress. You are now prepared to explore the different styles and methods of meditating with tarot cards to discover the best one for you.

Meditation signals your brain that it's time to get into the headspace for receiving messages through the stories in your tarot cards. You have alerted your roommates or family members that you are going into meditation, you have turned off devices or placed them on airplane mode. You have decided what tools or sacred objects you wish to include in your meditative tarot practice to set the mood, and any candles that relax your mind. You may wish to diffuse essential oils or dab a drop on your wrists or neck. To avoid potential skin irritation, use a carrier oil mixture with the essential oil of choice. Good kitchen oils such as coconut, olive, or sunflower oil work quite well. Use lavender to calm your mind, cinnamon for comfort, frankincense to invoke ancient energies, and cedarwood for grounding. Playing soft or relaxing music in the background further ignites the senses. If you are nervous about an impending question, brew a cup of chamomile tea before beginning. Each ritual item you incorporate seeks to create an even, balanced atmosphere for a successful outcome.

Simple Steps to Prepare Your Deck

Tarot cards are keepers of the profound energy of knowledge. The more we treat the deck with kindness, care, and respect as a sacred object, the more forthcoming it will be in working succinctly and easily with us. No matter how often you use your tarot deck(s), I recommend cleansing it to rid it of any negative energy or stagnation.

There are several ways to cleanse your deck. Use incense or herbs to smoke clear your deck. Direct the smoke over and around your deck by softly blowing the smoke several times, with a clear mind and heart.

Praying with your deck is another effective method of cleansing. One simple prayer or mantra at the beginning of using your tarot deck is "may the messages through these cards support my highest good" and at the end, "may all negativity leave my deck, and may it rest in the peace of its own wisdom until we meet again."

Place your deck in a soft cloth bag or a box with cleansing crystals. Selenite in particular is incredible for cleansing objects of all kinds. I keep one in a wooden box with my cards at all times. In addition to cleansing, it also connects with spirit guide energies. Other stones and crystals that are wonderful for enhancing psychic abilities include amethyst, clear quartz crystal, labradorite, moonstone, blue apatite, lapis lazuli, and azurite. Leave your deck out under the full moon. The moon's natural rays are effective at cleansing both tarot cards and any stones or crystals you may work with. Just leave them to bathe overnight on a windowsill; they will be ready to go the next day.

If you are an energy healer, you could use Reiki or other hands-on healing modalities. Channeling healing energies through your hands can provide an instant release of cluttered energies.

Drawing a Card

You will continue to advance your relationship with the tarot easily over time, but each time you pick up the deck to use it should be as if you are picking it up the first time, free of the energetic clutter of having been in other situations with other questions and other people.

I cannot understate the importance of treating your tarot decks as sacred tools. Our connection with any psychic tool increases the longer we work with them. It can be helpful to keep them nearby as often as possible, so they can consistently link up with our energy and be at the ready to perform.

Now comes the fun part. In tarot, there are several ways you can draw a card from the deck. You can shuffle the deck, cut it into three piles, then place them all back again, and draw from the top.

You can fan them out in a half circle and select a card that you feel most drawn to, or you can shuffle the cards and wait until one drops onto your lap.

There are countless ways to draw a card, but this last method is my favorite. I feel as though the cards are speaking their magic wisdom to me when I wait for a card to fall out of the deck on its own, while shuffling. And then I sit, eyes closed, the pulled card resting in my palms, and what blossoms is usually quite revealing. I've found that the more I combine tarot with meditation, the more in tune and grounded I feel within my body. In a more literal sense, the card gives me a focal point for when my mind wanders off to my never-ending to-do list or to the default auto-pilot irrational worries twisting up my mind as a busy business owner and mother of three.

Here are a couple more unique yet effective exercises to prepare for your meditative tarot practice. These are all suggestions to assist you in attaining another sort of access to the innate wisdom contained within the deck.

Choose Your Tarot Card Technique

Rifle through the tarot deck while it is face up. Choose one or two cards that inspire you, catch your attention, or you feel are speaking directly to you in the moment. When you have your cards chosen, sit back and study. Reflect on the images and the feelings the cards evoke. Ask yourself why you may have felt drawn to those particular cards. What might be going on in your life that caused you to choose them? If there are a handful of cards you continuously choose to focus on, that can be quite telling. I know I'm particularly drawn to the Empress from the major arcana. When I choose that card in meditation, it is as if she is speaking directly to me, filling my heart with nurturing comfort, love, and joy.

You can likewise choose a tarot card dependent on a specific subject that is on the top of the psyche. For instance, in the event that you are looking forward to bringing new love into your life, you may choose the Lovers or the Two of Cups simply because they inspire the emotions you would like to feel. Or if you are seeking to disconnect from the world, and retreat within, you may choose to meditate on the Hermit. The process of choosing is less about receiving big breakthrough messages and more about consoling the heart, validating our own life experiences, and studying in reflection until a sense of acceptance and peace emerges. Our ability to understand ourselves through the images and stories of tarot is truly a gift. Once you become familiar with the cards in this way, you can start picking up tarot spreads and using them with ease.

We can all personally identify with one or more cards in the tarot deck. When you consciously choose a few cards that you feel best represent you, who you are, and your personality, you can next study them and ask yourself why that may be so. Do they have particular qualities about them that you embody? What is it about those cards that represent you? I know I associate the Magician from the major arcana for my partner Troy, who has multiple talents and in his life and work has to juggle and balance many different facets of his personality. He's successful because of all of the ways in which he is equipped to perform in his life.

Similarly, rifle through the deck face-up and choose a few cards you feel repelled by or whose images confuse you or trigger anxious, scared, or sad feelings. In tarot, every card has both positive and negative sides. The positive surfaces through the innate wisdom they each hold. The more negative meaning surfaces usually to validate or confirm something you are already going through. For example, I used to be instantly triggered in a negative way by the Hierophant in the major arcana. In the beginning, I associated this card with religious authority, and not the good kind. For many years in my twenties, I disassociated with religion in general and especially the religious authority I had grown up believing I needed to follow without really knowing why. Eventually I grew to make peace with this card, realizing that it actually means "Holy One" and that there are some universal spiritual truths we can and should embrace and live by. In all of my years reading tarot, I have yet to have a "bad omen" or a premonition come through the tarot cards that caught me off guard. I like making friends with the cards that provoke fear or sadness because I feel I have the most to learn from them. They help me grow more comfortable with my own shadow side, and that is invaluable to me. I want to know all facets of my psyche and myself; it feels empowering to move through life understanding how I tick, and to embrace my imperfections, and emotional vulnerabilities.

Make your tarot practice a sacred ritual by laying out a beautiful cloth, and some stones or crystals, lighting a candle and then doing a tarot reading. When you enter into this sacred space with intention, you establish a routine way of working with your cards that spirit will more readily respond to. It's just another way of collaborating with the harmonizing forces of the universe.

CHAPTER FOUR

Meditation Techniques

Before any psychic practice and especially tarot, I encourage grounding and centering for protection. Here's a fun analogy for coffee drinkers: Engaging in a psychic practice without grounding is like leaving the house in the morning without your first cup of coffee. There is something for me personally about the ritual of making and drinking coffee that sets the tone for the entire day. I notice if it gets missed, and it affects my work performance and mood, and scatters my energy. Grounding lends consistency and focus to any psychic tool, technique, or discipline.

Grounding

There are many ways to ground for protection. Meditation is one way. Walking with bare feet on the earth, known as "earthing," is another, as is laying on the ground to take in the sky. Because I live in the Northern Hemisphere, I can't put my feet safely on the ground all year due to the weather. So I enjoy grounding indoors with meditation. Here is the outline for a simple and effective grounding meditation.

First, choose a place to sit where you can have both feet on the floor. Relax your posture, and your breath, moving the air in through your nose, and out through your mouth. Imagine golden cords of light extending from the soles of your feet all the way to the center of the earth. Breathe rhythmically. When you release your breath, move any unwanted or trapped energy down your grounding chords to the center of the earth, where it can safely be released and healed. The earth moves that recycled energy back up your body as it cleanses, renews, and restores you. Next, move that cleansed and restored energy up through your spinal column and out the top of your head through your crown chakra where it falls down around your body in a waterfall of protection. With your protective barrier in place, you can move your attention to your heart. Imagine opening your heart like the waves of the ocean, pulsing and rolling outward, expanding you. This is a wonderful first step. Your grounding, centering and protection is complete, and you are free to move on to other exercises.

One of the most common barriers to developing a meditative tarot practice is time, or the perceived lack of it. As a mother of three busy children, I absolutely can relate. I don't intend to inundate you with suggestions that set an unattainable expectation. Your practice needs to fit into your life, so it's an ongoing personal evaluation of both commitment and realistic goals.

One-Minute Tarot Meditation

The simplest, quickest meditation to prepare for a reading is to breathe, center yourself with your eyes closed, get in your body, and focus on the question while simultaneously shuffling your cards. This doesn't require more than a minute.

Choose three cards. At this time, they are in no special placement; they simply work together in harmony to deliver a message. Flip them over, and take a brief pause while absorbing each card, mentally noting the cards drawn without arriving at any conclusions just yet. For example, let's say you have drawn the Tower as one of your cards. Rather than reacting out of a negative prior assumption about that card, breathe into it a bit and ask yourself what you *really* feel about that card in relation to your question in the moment. Sometimes a hidden truth unexpectedly surfaces, such as secretly welcoming a sudden change that lets you now feel completely free to release something effective immediately. Refrain from making initial assumptions by returning to your breath and remaining a neutral observer until a more balanced perspective surfaces.

This is a form of meditation that encourages objectivity, levity, and careful observation and reflection. This swift meditative exercise enhances your ability to take information in quickly, and boosts your intuitive skills by reducing internal noise, which assists you in getting closer to the meaning of the cards for the moment you are in.

When you are finished with the meditation, breathe and ground again, releasing any unwanted energies and cutting ties with any cloudy emotional energy that surfaced so you can move on with your day. I highly recommend this exercise as a daily practice. It has the enhanced objective of clearing your mind and imprinting a potential energy flow or series of outcomes for the day.

While it is very tempting to reach for a guidebook or the internet to help with interpretations, I will always advise tarot enthusiasts to use their intuition first rather than have the interpretations of others projected onto a situation. I am all for building in book meanings and interpretations, but it's best to always first consider what you feel about the card rather than absorbing the insights of a book that doesn't know you or the situation you are asking about. You know you best. The card just as easily expresses itself through your intuition.

Thirty-Day Major Arcana Meditation

For those who appreciate a predictable and repeatable way to work with tarot and meditation, try out the thirty-day major arcana meditation. This daily exploration should not take more than ten minutes per day. The goal we are trying to achieve is to project our consciousness onto one selected tarot card per one meditation session. After the thirty days, you can extend the time allotted for this exercise. I find that the shorter the duration of the exercise, the less likely the analytical mind is to interfere with the process.

Separate out the twenty-two major arcana cards beginning with the Fool and ending with the World. Set the rest of your deck aside. Position the first card in front of your eyes. Adjust the distance so that you can observe all the details without any effort. Fixate your gaze on the card for a few seconds. Then close your eyes and on your inner vision attempt to recreate the image you were gazing at. Open your eyes again, and notice the differences between your inner image and the actual image of the card. You can repeat this several times, while gradually increasing the gazing period. Move on to the next card when you feel ready. Remember in the beginning to keep this daily meditation short—ten minutes maximum.

Through this exercise, you are teaching yourself to become a natural observer. No projections, no tensions, just an easy smooth flow of taking in the image in a space of total relaxation. Before long and without effort, you will have mastered the ability to take in the image and project it on the inner screen of your mind. The purpose is to assist you in focusing your inner eye and inner vision to reveal important and often private information about the card you were gazing at, or about yourself.

Symbolism Meditation

If you find yourself drawn to the symbols in the tarot rather than the people in the cards, this may be your go-to meditation. All seventy-eight tarot cards have symbols that represent certain facets of our lives. The meanings are steeped in the mystical, the metaphysical, spiritual, mythological, and historical aspects throughout time. The symbolism behind the tarot's artwork deepens the meaning of every card and how they interplay with each other in a reading. You may find tremendous strength in your own tarot practice through a meditative study on the symbols.

Prepare your space and deck in your preferred method. Shuffle and draw a few cards or pick a few to which you're drawn. Notice what symbols stand out to you, and look for any similarities between the symbols in each of the cards drawn. Note any patterns. Avoid the temptation to look up any symbol meanings, at least for now. This exercise is about developing your intuition and connection with each card.

Look at and study the artwork. Here are questions to ask yourself as it relates to the symbols:

1. What feelings do the colors evoke?
2. If there is a focal point in the artwork, why do you think that is?
3. What symbols do you see?
4. Are there people? If so, how are they interacting with the symbols? What do you feel that means?
5. What actions are happening, or not happening?
6. Are there animals or plants?

Study the card or cards for at least five full minutes. Let your own insights and ideas percolate. Then write them down without editing or judging yourself. Some of the symbolism you may know, but it's just as possible that you didn't grow up learning mythology or religion and may not be familiar with them. That's okay. Just do the best you can. Write down what you think the card means based entirely upon its symbols and the artwork.

Momentarily put your findings away and go about your day. The next day, look up the different meanings of the symbols you noticed in the artwork. Compare, contrast, and add any additional meanings that feel resonant to your journal or notebook. If it's helpful, use a different colored ink to represent the "book meanings" of the symbols. There are bound to be differences, but don't let it intimidate you. That doesn't mean you are wrong; it's just a different perspective, and it's valuable to incorporate multiple interpretations. Because the symbols are universal and represent common aspects of the human condition and spiritual doorways or milestones we all go through, your own personal experiences of the symbols can add a depth that using only a book reference cannot provide. Waking up the symbols within you is like a remembrance of something familiar, waking up to knowledge that you've held within for lifetimes.

Write a message to yourself about this card's meaning, based upon your own intuition. Revisit this anytime you feel called to, or when you're confused about how the card fits into the story a reading is trying to tell you.

Join the Tarot Story Meditation

This meditative exercise can be used for each card in the entire tarot deck. It is especially helpful for times when you are stuck or confused about a particular tarot card meaning as it relates to your question. One of the most frustrating experiences with tarot can be when you aren't able to make the meaning connection. Don't fret! There is a way to handle this moment with grace and ease. Before collapsing the cards in angst, pause to do this exercise first and see if it makes a difference. This meditation exercise will allow you to join the story in any of the cards you are struggling with or wish to grow closer to and understand more deeply. It is similar to the path Alice takes through the looking glass, or the children in the *Narnia* book series go through when they enter the magical otherworld through the coat closet. Allowing yourself to join the story of the cards by becoming the characters in them allows you to learn all about what's happening in the scene and how it relates to you. This process slows down the brain synapses that connect thoughts, helping you to read between the lines a bit better on the meaning of the card. Hopefully it will help you block out unnecessary emotional interference, allowing the connection to the card in your heart and mind.

First, close your eyes and immediately move your thoughts into your body. Slow down your breathing and become consciously aware of the air moving in and out of your body. As you take in air, imagine the oxygen filling it to be healing and rejuvenating. With each breath, you feel calm, centered, and focused. What's more, you feel a sense of relaxation channeling through the frame of your body as you exhale. Allow this relaxation to sweep over your head, shoulders, torso, arms, neck, hips, legs, and feet, and feel the unwinding moving through right down to the tips of your feet or toes. Experience this in each cell of your body. This initial breathing exercise should take no more than a few minutes. Now open your eyes and concentrate on the card(s) you drew. For a moment, just rest easy in the space with the card. Pay attention to any musings pulsing through your consciousness and psyche; just watch and observe, as if they are just gliding in and out of your thoughts without attachment. Keep your breath slow and steady. Become more aware of the card(s) before you now. Imagine the cards becoming bigger and bigger before you, until the figures and symbols become life-sized in your vision. Join the story by taking a step into the card itself and look around there. Imagine you are in the story of the card; you are becoming a part of it. You get to observe what's going on within the scene with the characters, symbols, or landscape. Experience it all for yourself. What's happening when you enter the scene? Is there anyone there with you? Notice how it feels and what interactions take place. Observe what you feel, hear, and sense. Take in a full breath and feel the air and sunshine surrounding it.

Become one of the characters or symbols in the card. Notice how it feels to join the story rather than trying to understand the card from an objective place. How do you proceed or act being a character or symbol in the card? Take a few notes as new insights begin to emerge from merging with and becoming a part of the story in this particular card. Notice how your frame of mind is shifting, as you are becoming the characters in the card. If you are still feeling confused, begin to speak or take notes and write thoughts as if you are that figure, in that card. Become the character and allow your imagination to take hold. This can be a playful experiment, and you may be surprised at how effective it is. Discern what you need from the scene or story in the card to feel whole and complete again. Speak or write that down. Be specific with your dialogue with the characters, or with yourself, to best understand what is happening through this experience. Be clear about what you are asking the card to provide for you.

Take one more pause to look around you. Be aware of what it is in that scene that would make you feel better or give you energy. Observe any surfacing emotions or feelings. Write them down. Allow yourself to change or manipulate the story as you see fit in order for the scene you are experiencing to go the way you want it to. Take note of the ways in which you consciously or unconsciously determined the scene needed to change for you to be okay with the card's story. These modifications are your sub-conscious mind revealing its desires, needs, wishes, or wants in real life circumstances. Allow this awareness to fuel your actions and decisions in real time.

Be present once more with the images and symbols of the card as it begins to decrease in size, and you come back out of it, back into the room, back into your own body. With each breath now, you slowly return. Gaze carefully at the card again. Notice what other insights may be coming to you now, that hadn't previously.

Take time to journal or write down what you felt or experienced through this exercise. You can come back anytime to this same exercise with a card you'd like to get closer to and understand from another perspective. All it takes is some patience and a little imagination.

Here are a few hand-selected major arcana cards you might wish to use with this tarot meditation technique. These are just a few suggestions. I've personally found it useful to begin with the twenty-two major arcana when joining the stories of the cards and expanding from there. I encourage you to use your own intuition and your personal interpretations of the cards to lead you on your journeys into the unknown.

The Empress: Learn more about your capacity for unconditional love, and your own gentle nurturing gifts. Who in life do you need to heal relationships with? How can you take a gentle yet firm approach? What right now is blocking your heart center?

The Emperor: Explore your own inner willpower and challenging our ability to take action and make strong decisions, even when faced with obstacles. Where in life do you need more assertiveness or action? How can you best take the lead to move a situation forward? Where do you need to solve problems? Don't be afraid to assert yourself.

The Hierophant: Receive sound guidance in the form of universal truths. What aspect of life have you been resisting or ignoring, hoping it would resolve itself? Imagine a wise, grounded master offering you solutions and direction. No need to reinvent the wheel with the wisdom in this card. Go to this master and discover time-honored ways of doing things.

The Lovers: Explore the bonds of your relationships as well as their boundaries and limits. What do you need to do to improve them or let them go? This is the time to be fully honest with yourself and see the relationship(s) as they really are. Listen closely to a partner's needs, desires, and wishes and emerge with a stronger perspective. Sort out how you can resolve any issues between you. If you are not in a relationship, use this exercise to further understand your relationship with yourself—the most important relationship of all.

The Star: Explore freely your own wishes and dreams for the future. What dreams have you forsaken? Why? Do you feel afraid of failure? Are you telling yourself untruths? Find ways through this card to restore faith in yourself. Reimagine a pathway forward that includes your dreams.

The Sun: Explore feeling more connected to your own purpose, or to uplift your spirits when you are low. What area of life seems to dim your light? What can you do to diminish negative influences, barriers, or blocks to success, and what steps can you take to replenish your soul's path?

CHAPTER FIVE

Journal Prompts and Exercises

Journaling is a common ritual activity advocated in many spiritual practices. When consistently practiced over a certain period of time, the act of record keeping in the form of journaling produces an important function: the act of record keeping allows you to focus and settle into your thoughts in a very complete way. Journaling is a chance to record any thoughts or inspiration that come up during your meditation and tarot practice. Your journal becomes your own personal grimoire and a sort of esoteric code language between you and your spirit allies and guides. It is a fabulously flexible tool, in that you may choose to keep track through written word, drawings, artwork, using colors, objects from nature, designs, or whatever you want to keep a record that represents your experiences. Some things may be best represented abstractly, while other tarot impressions will be best expressed through words.

Journaling may not seem like meditation, but it's actually a rather powerful form of it. Often once pen meets paper, something magical can happen in that the insights or thoughts begin to take a form and shape unto their own and spontaneously expand upon what you were originally intending to write. Those who have a particular affinity for the spoken or written word may find this activity fits like a glove. However, even if you don't consider yourself a wordsmith, it doesn't matter—the most important thing is to do it in some form.

Your journal doesn't need to be anything fancy. You can choose anything from a plain spiraled school notebook to a composition book, to a leather-bound or handmade journal. The best choice is whatever inspires you to use it. Adorn, decorate, or draw pictures on the front if you wish. I also find that certain writing utensils are more pleasing to use than others. I like using an ink-filled fountain pen, as it lends a smoothness to the writing experience and creates beautiful pictures and letters. I prefer not to use a pencil, since often the lead writing can fade over time. Journaling is a pretty popular and trendy activity these days, so specialty gift stores and boutiques as well as bookstores often have them in stock.

When organized over time, your journal will begin to reveal certain patterns that may be in the form of common symbols or repetitive suits, cards, or numbers that show up, or similar themes in the readings themselves. Journaling as a tracking method showcases how the cycles and patterns of your life and events are affecting you, giving you invaluable leverage. Through time, you may see familiar patterns you are uncomfortable with and wish to change. This tracking system can assist you in better predicting various outcomes for yourself in your life, because you begin to understand the cycles you move through on a regular basis. In addition, this link to the consistent or repetitive themes assists you in establishing a working code language that spirit is attempting to relay on to you through the cards. Each of us has a co-creative team of spirits who inevitably toss in their two cents when asked, and you can use tarot to develop a language to better understand their messages for you.

Journal Prompts for Your Meditative Tarot Practice

These questions are meant to be a starting point for you, especially in the event you've never journaled before. You don't need to use all of the questions; you can hand select the ones that feel like a good fit. This journal exercise is used after you have drawn cards. No particular format or tarot spread is required to use these prompts.

Name the cards in the tarot spread and their placements. If you aren't using a tarot spread, just write down the cards in order. Make note of how many major arcana cards there are. Make note of how many minor arcana cards there are.

- Is there more than one card in the same suit?
- What is the distribution of elements, i.e. earth, air, fire, water cards? What might that mean given my life situation?
- Are there any repetitive numbers? What do those numbers represent?
- Are there repetitive colors, symbols, or themes?
- How might the cards reflect what is happening in my life?
- What is my intuition telling me about the pictures in the cards?
- What cards are confusing me?
- Write down your first impression about the cards drawn.
- Jot down any other impressions whether or not they are represented by the cards.
- What final conclusion can I come to for today from the tarot spread?

Basic Meditative Tarot Journaling Exercise

This exercise is how I teach all beginning tarot students. Come back to this exercise as a basic approach to connect yourself to the cards you draw in a contemplative way. It involves a simple med-itative exercise where you gaze at one card at a time and ask the following questions for each:

1. What emotions does this image evoke within me?
2. What might the story in this card be telling me?
3. What are one or two words I can associate with this card?
4. Tie everything together in a one-sentence message the cards are revealing.

For the artistically inclined, you can begin a drawing journal: trace or draw the cards free hand. In this exercise, the cards can move through you much like a muse, inspiring you with their own wisdom. In addition, there are many online stores that sell individual sheets or complete coloring books of blank tarot cards. A wonderful meditation is to spend time with markers, paints, or colored pencils and either create your own colorful palette or attempt to replicate the colors in the original Waite-Smith tarot deck. When the tarot cards move through you in this sensual way, you become much more intimately connected to them.

Free Writing Exercise

Each time you do this exercise, be sure to clear your deck and pre-pare properly to clear any previous energy. After cleansing, shuffle your deck using your preferred method. Select a card either randomly or spread them out and select one you are led to. Lay the card out in front of you.

Scan the guidebook that came with your deck to the relevant page. Read the interpretation or keywords but don't try to memo-rize or completely absorb it; just read it through, lightly taking in the information. Next, set a timer for five minutes. Glance at the card again, then pick up your pen and start writing. Start the timer when you begin writing what initially comes to mind.

Now write whatever comes to mind without stopping, no editing allowed. Although it may seem like what you write doesn't make any sense, this writing style frees you up to let thoughts bubble up that normally you might dismiss as your imagination or a wandering thought. Write everything down; the analysis can come later. The subconscious and unconscious mind is set free to reveal to you what may have previously been hidden from view. Surprising or unexpected information may surface, shifting your mindset or perspective.

When the five minutes are up, put your pen down and walk away from the exercise. Come back and read it later, and highlight or underline things that feel resonant or supportive in the moment. Notice where you have written things you don't recall or that feel as if they came from another place.

Card Combinations Journal Exercise

This meditative journaling exercise is best done with tarot spreads of more than one card. We can build in plenty more meaning when we notice the card combinations; the archetypes, numbers, suits, symbols, and repetitive themes. The energy of the dominant element in the minor arcana can significantly override the individual card meanings, so it's best to note those in your journal. For example, if you draw mostly cups (emotion and imagination) during a reading but you usually process your life through the lens of logic, assume this situation might be more emotionally troubling than you initially anticipated. Allow the repetition in the card themes to pierce your own awareness, driving your internal processing. You don't want to force it, but you also can reflect in your journal and write down how this actually may be affecting you more emotionally than you realized. By contrast, if you draw more swords cards (air, of the mind) but you typically feel your way intuitively through situations, you may be now guided to add logic to what you are feeling or do some reality testing before assuming based on emotion alone what is happening around your question.

Also, you can consider the numbers on the cards as a great way to apply a timeline to a question. The lower the numbers in your reading, the more likely you are to be closer to the beginning of a situation reaching resolution. For example, if you spot several aces or numbered cards 1 through 3, you can mentally note that this situation may take a bit longer to reach a conclusion or closure. If you draw multiple cards with the numbers 4 through 6, you can rest assured you are no longer at the beginning of the road to your destination, you are mid-way, and there is still time to change course or make a needed change to arrive at the destination you are seeking. If you draw mostly numbers 7 through 10, accept that you are further along a path than you may have realized; use this knowledge to your advantage and begin making plans for what's next.

Similarly with the major arcana, pay attention to the atmosphere of the cards drawn. The archetypes have tones ranging from clear and light to neutral to dark, depending on the cards. If you find yourself in the midst of cards whose characteristics and behaviors trigger more of your shadow, slow down to reflect on this important revelation. No one can reasonably draw the Death or the Tower cards without pausing to wonder what's amiss in life, no matter how startling it may be to realize. You can ponder what you might be avoiding, ignoring, or resisting that needs more of your attention right now. If you've been avoiding facing your own inner storm or dark night of the soul, your tarot cards may be forcing the issue, assisting you in dealing with what's happening in an honest and more direct fashion. Another card, the Moon, definitely speaks to your inner depths and begs you to deal with a situation you may have stifled or stuffed inside. The nudges are strong and unavoidable. The sobering truth is the situation will still be there, whether or not you choose to deal with it in the moment—no time like the present!

On the other hand, if you draw more than one archetype that appears more bright or neutral such as the Sun, the Hanged Man, the Wheel of Fortune, Temperance, or the World, the patterns through them suggest a brighter time or cycle of your life. Allow the good energy of them to permeate your heart and soul. Bring the mood-lifting messages into your heart. Write down how the combination of cards makes you feel about the current life situation in question. Do you feel more optimistic about your options? You can move forward now centered in the awareness of a good outcome and the confidence to persevere through whatever obstacles may appear.

CHAPTER SIX

Deciphering Messages

Carefully framing your question at the beginning of your tarot reading helps you more properly decipher the messages they reveal. For daily readings, you can simply ask, "What do I need to know today?" or "What is my card for the day?" When working with a tarot spread, choose one specific area of your life at a time. It is best to assume 100 percent responsibility for your choices. For example, rather than asking the cards "What should I do?" or "Will this ever work out?," try "What can I do to improve this situation?" or "What can I do differently to achieve my goals?" You will get much more bang for your buck when you walk into your readings with an automatic assumption you are in charge of your life and that through the power of free will, you will determine the best outcome. When you follow the guidance presented in the cards, it can lead to beautiful outcomes.

The good news and the bad news about reading tarot cards is exactly the same. Each time you draw cards, they may mean something different depending on the context of the question. This can make tarot appear unreliable at times, but it is this same quality that makes it a fabulously rich, deep, and flexible tool. Knowing how to navigate the changeable meanings in the tarot takes a centered and consistent practice of patient discovery.

I can draw the Queen of Pentacles in one reading to signify an authority figure in my life only to draw it another time to represent qualities and characteristics within myself that are being revealed. The Lovers card in one particular spread may be related to healing my relationship with my significant other and in another be about how I need to balance my conscious and subconscious mind, masculine and feminine sides of myself, or deal directly with how I am approaching my relationships. The Tower card in one reading may mean something is ready to come to an end in my life and it's time to take immediate action for change, and in the next can affirm something surprising is happening to me that I have no control over.

Here's an interesting consideration, one worth paying attention to: When one or more of the major arcana cards surface in a reading, they carry a bit of additional weight to the message, punctuating the situation in question more potently than the minor arcana. It's a way of confirming a more significant issue or area of life you are asking about. When you draw a major arcana card, note that it will likely be the reading's focal point. The major arcana is the through line of the story, and the minor arcana fills in the background details. Minor arcana cards are fluid and changeable parts of our life experiences. When primarily minor arcana cards are drawn in a spread, I typically encourage readers to let a little time pass and then ask the same question another day to see if anything has changed. Sometimes, depending on how things have evolved, the course of action or guidance will have changed. Minor arcana cards can track ongoing movement and change through a life situation rather easily and reveal the progress.

We are multisensory beings. During our meditation and tarot practice, our intuition works together in tandem with our third eye, our sixth sense, our logical mind, and our natural psychic abilities. When we draw tarot cards, there are times we can access information in the form of additional symbols, messages, voices in our head, sensations, feelings, and *a-ha!* moments. It's the culmination of this multi-layered experience that brings about a well-rounded tarot message. If you receive messages but don't immediately know what they are, it's okay to write them down to revisit at a later time. There are several apps and online resources you can use to further clarify any additional information you may be receiving.

Putting It All Together

The first step is always to do your grounding and prepare the space properly, including any necessary cleansing and engagement in your preferred ritual activities. Next, ask a question and lay out tarot cards in sequence according to a spread or at random. After that, choose one of the meditation exercises in this book and offer your third eye and intuition the chance to bring into your awareness the next approach to absorb the meanings of the cards as a whole. In other words, the cards inevitably have a story to show you; if you scan the cards all together, you can gather a visual impression, similar to a scene from a film. In your journal, write your first impressions on what the story might be, including all the cards together. Note whether the story tone seems heavy, emotional, light, fun, somber, exciting, warning, adventurous, inspiring, and so on. Next, back up and dissect each card one at a time. Layering in additional interpretations after you first take in the story chapter adds a certain depth that over time you may grow to appreciate. Once you have added in book meanings, you can sit back in a reflective space and allow any further guidance to emerge. There's no need to worry about where it is coming from—simply allowing this extra beat at the end can make a tremendous difference in the clarity of the reading itself.

CHAPTER SEVEN

Sacred Wisdom Embedded in the Tarot

The tarot is embedded with hundreds of years' worth of gathered esoteric knowledge, mysticism, and is periodically encoded with Egyptian hieroglyphs, references to ancient traditions such as the Kabbalah and astrology, and Hebrew symbols. An early ninety-seven-card Florentine deck also incorporated extra trumps whose names were drawn from the three theological virtues (Faith, Hope, Charity), the four elements, and twelve signs of the zodiac. As the deck evolved, obviously the creators of the day took free license to add content they considered valuable and discarded the rest. The modern tarot deck is a conglomeration of cherry-picked symbolism, spiritual wisdom, and ideas gathered over time.

Tarot's sacred wisdom is perhaps most revealed through the Fool's Journey of the major arcana. There are philosophical leanings throughout the entire tarot, but they are particularly prevalent in the twenty-two archetypes, as they portray the journey we as human beings embark on through life. It's the one we walk from the time we are born until we die. They challenge us to look deeper at how we embody the wisdom of the cardinal virtues of prudence, temperance, courage, and justice.

Through the major arcana, we are staring into the face of our own moral courage, selfless pursuits, contributions, selfish aims, transitions, relationships, choices, trappings, celebrations, ambitions, achievements, and limitations, where we are under the thumb of oppressive patriarchal systems, and where the world may seem stacked against us. At different stages of life, we are faced with the same challenges and opportunities the characters in the major arcana go through, leaving us with the brutal recognition that we have but one life to fulfill what we are here to do.

The major arcana offers us a series of sobering reminders, pressing into us the realities and consequences of a life course well- or ill-charted. Daring to look into the truth of the faces and symbols of those cards, we are either enhanced by their wise clear guidance or slip into denial, unwilling to heed their wisdom. In this sense, it takes a certain bravery to look into them closely, but they can act as divine portals that extract us from ruts and old patterns; assisting us in shifting our perspective or embracing needed change.

Like the Fool, we begin this journey and embark on a path of which we don't yet know the outcome. Our clues to the next phase or chapter of our lives exist amongst the major arcana's figures. These figures sometimes represent those who we merge with on our path, sometimes helping, other times hindering us depending on their own intent and motivations. They are sometimes harsh realizations that we have strayed from a virtuous path through vanity or greed (the Devil), they lend us permission to tap into and follow our dreams (the Star), they give us strong hints to much needed albeit dramatic life changes (the Tower), they urge us to check in with our relationships (the Lovers), they offer us balance and grace in times of uncertainty (Temperance), they remind us not to reinvent the wheel, but to follow time-honored truths

(Justice), they tell us when the world is closing in and it's time to retreat (the Hermit), and they show us when a cycle of phase of our lives is complete (the World), for starters.

The elevated level of wisdom tarot provides our lives is invaluable: a daily dose of counsel that provides much-needed focus that helps us combat the wild and unpredictable mood swings of the world we live in. Tarot is rich with an encoded wisdom, invented over time, and assigned to each of the 78 cards. Although the invented meanings evolved throughout history, it is difficult to deny its universal application relative to the human condition. As a whole, it is a system for describing opportunities or challenges to aspirations and emotional concerns.

Tarot is loaded with universal mythological and folk symbolism yet remains fluid enough for us to generate our own personal mythology through our use of them. We are, after all, each a living myth, this life revealing our own allegorical narrative while we simultaneously battle our own demons against the backdrop of an evolving world. Together, we are the product of the times we live in, becoming a collective expression of stories, history, cultural traditions, and religious conditioning. Tarot will always allow us to connect to that myth and that story to assist us in potential course correction. Through the major arcana, we learn about and create our own stories. It is important to adapt the narrative against the backdrop of more modern times. And underneath societal evolution are universal human characteristics, traits, emotions, and behaviors: love, jealousy, greed, risk, suffering, grief, ambition, mental confusion, and happiness are all some examples.

When you ask a question to the tarot and receive guidance that you weren't expecting, your outlook is broadened. Tarot is exacting in its ability to give you what you need rather than what you want, or at the least cuts through the overly confident voice inside your head that in fact may be leading you astray. Give tarot the chance to show you what aspect or angle of a life situation you may be missing, and you'll open the door of a new possibility if not a deeper truth. Although the interpretations for the cards are inevitably in the eye of the beholder, you still cannot force the cards you want to surface. You must accept the cards you've drawn. It's like the good friend who won't say what you want to hear to avoid hurting your feelings. They instead reflect something more authentic and real. Sometimes it's a truth we aren't willing to see, but it can be the most pivotal guidance we didn't realize we had been looking for.

A Tool for Healing

We have all at times been woken up in the middle of the night feeling anxious or unable to stop our mind from spinning. Whether it's because of a relationship, personal, work-related, or financial issue, we all go through so much in our lives, making it too easy to neglect our own personal healing processes. Tarot can have an impact on our healing by providing much needed insight or direction, or it can spark an emotional release. It's the kind, understanding, and nonjudgmental best friend you can lean on for clarity.

We are in the midst of an onslaught of intense systemic change in our society. Staying informed and taking action are ways in which we can respond to this change. At times, the empathy fatigue can overwhelm us, leaving us feeling frayed and exhausted. Tarot can help us understand all the forces at play in our world and what we can do to help.

Tarot can also get us out of our heads and assist us to powerfully shifting the narrative of our lives. It can help us understand ourselves in a new way that can be therapeutic and allow us to understand how we make the decisions we make and why we behave the way we do. We can clearly see what we are going through and whether it is being driven by anxiety, avoidance, or resistance to hopefully transform the space into one of receptivity and acceptance. In periods of emotional turmoil, it is often difficult to see through the pain. Once the emotion calms, tarot's wisdom can bring us to a more objective outlook, drawing in otherwise unavailable helpful guidance. That said, connecting with tarot in this way is best done in an emotionally neutral space. In other words, it is best to first move through the emotion or moment of grief before digging out your deck. For those who have a difficult time navigating situations from a balanced emotional space, tarot can be especially important. If you find yourself triggered or reactive to things, tarot can help you better manage your own reactions to things, offering a safe haven of support. We can better shed past patterning and old karmic cycles, allowing us to navigate fears and traumas with clarity.

Calming Meditation and Healing Tarot Spread

Gather your ritual items: any props, stones, crystals, candles, or incense. Do your grounding exercise or meditation. From a neutral emotional space, shuffle your tarot deck, and divide into three piles face down.

Come into a comfortable sitting position. Bring to mind something difficult you are going through. It may be of benefit to choose something moderately difficult rather than the most difficult, as is practicing with this exercise in moderation first, until you become comfortable with it. If you feel the desire to push that difficulty away, just breathe and relax into the surfacing discomfort.

Start by breathing deeply in through your nose and out through your mouth a few times. Invite into your awareness a master, guide, or being of light who can protect you in a blanket of love and security. You could imagine a big cloud of compassion or a waterfall of protective light—whatever feels most loving and kind. Imagine this figure or image is holding you in a warm embrace.

Now turn fully toward your difficulty. Face it head on. There is no need to be afraid. Feel the master or guide enveloping you and speaking kindly to you: "You are okay, you are loved. You are not alone, and you will get through this. We will help you." Receive this loving support and nurturing as many times as you need as your mind and body begin to soothe and calm.

Remain in this meditation until you feel yourself settling in to a more smooth psychological state. Your sympathetic nervous system is firing off signals that you can physiologically relax. Feel your body releasing any tension or pain as a result of the discomfort. Open your eyes, and using your intuition, choose one of the three piles of tarot cards. These cards become your guide, providing any additional meaningful emotional support.

Place your cards in the following positions:

One: Where do I need to be more gentle with myself right now?

Two: How can I best move through this situation with grace?

Three: Is there something I am not seeing clearly about what happened?

Four: How might I best approach this situation for my own highest good?

Five: What am I learning about myself right now?

Six: What am I currently healing?

Seven: What else do I need to continue the healing process?

Eight: What do I need to help me move forward?

The use of a tarot spread is a wonderful way to gather information around a current life situation. While I don't regularly use tarot spreads, I love them on the back end of emotionally charged situations because they allow us the opportunity to lift a bit of the burden and let the spread and the cards do the heavy lifting. This tarot spread is wonderful for contemplating and healing from a difficult emotionally traumatic situation.

CHAPTER EIGHT

Integrating Tarot, Astrology, and Meditation

Astrology and tarot are intricately interlinked in a relationship that lends further layers of meaning to your own tarot readings. We can meditate on the astrological correlations in the cards, which add a rich depth to any tarot reading. There are twelve major arcana cards associated directly with zodiac signs and ten that correspond with the planets. The zodiac signs have one of four elements: air (Gemini, Libra, Aquarius), fire (Aries, Leo, Sagittarius), earth (Taurus, Virgo, Capricorn), and water (Cancer, Scorpio, Pisces). The air element governs the areas of thought, the intellect, communication, and the mind. The fire element is what drives our ambitions, sparks impulsive action, motivates us, and creates a warm inspiring tone. The earth element embodies grounded, steady, loyal, slow to change, methodical, and dependable characteristics. The water element portrays the qualities of empathy, sensitivity, intuition, imagination, and creativity.

Each zodiac sign also exhibits one of three qualities. Cardinal signs (Aries, Cancer, Libra, Capricorn) represent the initiators; they aren't about to wait around for something to happen, they are making things happen. Fixed signs (Taurus, Leo, Scorpio, Aquarius) signs are often less willing to take a risk but are the most loyal and steadfast of the zodiac. Mutable signs (Gemini, Virgo, Sagittarius, Pisces) are the more spontaneous, flexible, and adventurous members of the zodiac.

When these twelve major arcana surface during tarot readings, you can reflect on the sign, element, and quality of the card. For example, if you draw the Emperor, and we know Aries is the cardinal fire sign that rules this card, we can deduce that the Emperor is likely to represent us or somebody in our lives who embodies the characteristics of fire: assertive, active, aggressive, strong-willed, able to adequately regulate emotion, and moving through life with a "ready, set, go" mentality. In contrast, when we draw the Hermit, we know that the mutable earth sign Virgo is associated with it. The earth element is grounded, steady, focused, reliable, and with a fair amount of staying power. Earth signs are often the salt of the earth sorts of people, dependable and organized. So with the Hermit and Virgo's mutable quality, we can naturally decipher that this card represents something within that is flexible and changeable and at the same time loyal and hardworking. Add this quality to the meaning of the Hermit, and it unlocks a nuanced way of digging deeper into our interpretations. Multifaceted avenues of exploration make tarot a never-ending study.

For a simple exercise, rifle through the deck and locate the major arcana card that represents your own zodiac (or Sun) sign based on the key below. Reflect on the element and the quality as it relates to your own particular card. As you become a more seasoned tarot artist and reader who has the basic skills mastered, you can include additional layers of meaning.

Sign	Element	Quality	Tarot Card
Aries	Fire	Cardinal	The Emperor and the Tower
Taurus	Earth	Fixed	The Empress and the Hierophant
Gemini	Air	Mutable	The Lovers and the Magician
Cancer	Water	Cardinal	The Chariot, the High Priestess, the Moon
Leo	Fire	Fixed	The Sun and Strength
Virgo	Earth	Mutable	The Hermit
Libra	Air	Cardinal	Justice
Scorpio	Water	Fixed	Death, Judgement
Sagittarius	Fire	Mutable	Temperance and Wheel of Fortune
Capricorn	Earth	Cardinal	The Devil and the World
Aquarius	Air	Fixed	The Star and the Fool
Pisces	Water	Mutable	The Hanged Man

The twenty-two major arcana cards are each ruled by a planet. The planets in astrology correlate with archetypes and myths, similar to the major arcana. Use the additional characteristics and behaviors of the planets to deepen your understanding of the cards they rule.

The Fool and the Star: Ruled by Uranus, the planet of change, innovation, technology, and liberation, this planet supports our initiatives, our impulses, and gives us the motivation to change course.

The Magician, the Hermit, and the Lovers: Ruled by Mercury, the planet of the mind, it is related to our ability to manifest our ideas into form, and use our power of will effectively.

The High Priestess, the Chariot, and the Moon: Ruled by the Moon, the planet of intuitive vision and psychic abilities, this planet guides us to access our own inner vision and awareness.

The Empress, the Hierophant, and Justice: Ruled by Venus, the planet of love, sensuality, pleasure, and compassion, where we are guided to tend to our hearts, our creature comforts, our sexuality, and tending to the needs of others in our lives.

The Hanged Man: Ruled by Neptune, which governs dreams, psychic experiences, creative pursuits, and the mystical realm. This planet guides our inner vision, and supports our mystical and cosmic connections.

Wheel of Fortune and Temperance: Ruled by Jupiter, which embodies expansion through connection to cosmic laws, releasing ourselves into the wholeness of the universe, and the role we play within it.

The Emperor and the Tower: Ruled by Mars, the planet of upheaval, dramatic change, and sudden impact, we are often tossed into uncontrollable situations and encouraged to brace ourselves for the unexpected.

Strength and the Sun: Ruled by the Sun, the planet of self-realization and the ego, we are urged to direct our focus and energies to our own ability to self-actualize and press into our capacity for becoming in the world.

Death and Judgement: Ruled by Pluto, the penetrating planet of deep transformation. No stone is left unturned, no secrets hidden; to move forward, we must face the truth and deal with it.

The Devil and the World: Ruled by Saturn, the planet of discipline and self-mastery. To succeed, we often need a carefully constructed plan of action and the willpower to follow through.

For the next meditation, have your twenty-two major arcana cards set aside. For easy access, consider laying them all out in rows in order from the Fool (0) to the World (21).

Tarotstrology Meditation

This is a meditation to assist with our mind's natural powers of manifestation. Imagining how we would like to resolve an issue, and entertaining what we would like the outcome to be, can spark our intuition, and ignite the collaborative forces of the universe. Presuming that the universe is conspiring on our behalf is a wise mental habit.

Still your mind by taking ten nice slow, deep breaths. Breathing in this manner grounds and centers your attention, preparing your mind to absorb new information. Ask your mind to release any unnecessary thoughts. Invite your body to release all physical tension. Open your whole being into a more smooth, relaxed state.

Now bring to mind an area of concern or a question for your personal life path. Notice which of the following areas your question falls into: career, relationships, money, health, or spirituality.

1. Select one major arcana card whose image best resembles the situation in question.
2. Reflect on the element, quality, or planet that is associated with that card.
3. Select one major arcana card whose story showcases what you would like the outcome or resolution of that situation to be.
4. Reflect on the element, quality, or planet that is associated with that card.
5. Select one major arcana card that best portrays one action step you can take toward healing the situation or that represents what part of yourself you are calling on to accomplish what's next.
6. Reflect on the element, quality, or planet that is associated with that card.

Now close your eyes, and reconnect to your breath, and imagine a scenario where the outcome is what you see. Notice how your life has changed or adjusted to beautifully open to you to this new possibility and outcome. When you open your eyes, take all of the excitement you are feeling about this potential outcome and journal what you felt or saw with your inner vision.

CHAPTER NINE

Building a Relationship with Your Tarot Deck

Deepening your relationship with the tarot is a process enhanced by an ongoing practice of getting acquainted with the images you feel drawn to and that resonate with you the most, in addition to the cards you find off-putting. The images, scenarios, and archetypes dwell deep within our psyches and reveal to us our deepest fears, wishes, and needs. Establishing a bond with your tarot cards can open doorways of deeper connection with yourself and the Divine.

I recall a time in my life when tarot was the only friend I could connect with. I was pregnant with my third child, nursing a toddler, chasing after an eight-year-old, and trying to maintain some sense of mental balance through it all. It often was the one thing that brought me through my day unscathed by life's chaotic realities. Tarot helped me to break up the monotony of life as a busy mother. Stopping all activities helped alleviate the dull ache of wear and tear on my body and freed my mind to source the poetry of the universe, which tarot is to me. It was my moment to connect with my own heart, mind, and soul. I still see this tool in the same ways even now, though my uses of tarot have become perhaps a bit more sophisticated. Perhaps you aren't a mother but you have a busy career or hectic lifestyle. Tarot offers a way to hit the pause button, if even for a moment.

When you work with the tarot, you begin to realize the power in the bond you share that has tremendous potential to develop and grow over time. It is always ready and willing to connect with you when you are open and ready to connect with it.

I recall the moment when I felt myself merge with the deck in a new way, moving beyond rote memorization and book interpretations. It happened after about a decade of consistently reading, studying, and connecting with my cards. I would be having a conversation with someone or in a phone reading with a client, and suddenly a tarot card image would spontaneously pop into my mind. Sometimes it was an insight for me, and at other times it was for the person I was having a chat with. At the time I didn't know what to do when it happened, but later I realized there was such an integration happening with this mystical tool that it had begun to merge with the core of my very being. I obviously couldn't deny its magic, so I determined that it was important to pay attention to the ways in which my deck was connecting to and through me whether or not I had the actual deck in my hands.

My story illustrates the interesting and curious relationship you'll build with a seemingly inanimate object. The movement of the energetic bond you establish with your deck will astound you. You'll suddenly feel it and potentially grow to understand this narrative: It isn't really the cards that are speaking to and through you; they are simply placeholders for inherent universal and mystical knowledge we all have access to. This is why the encouragement to study them as if they are characters in your life is relevant; they are living, breathing wisdom keepers, connectors to a momentary lightning bolt of clarity, shapeshifters revealing fresh insights, and comrades offering us the most honest depiction of what we are going through and what to do about it.

Welcoming a New Deck

Use this particular exercise when you first acquire a new deck. It can be a simple, yet effective way of getting acquainted, similar to meeting a new friend. First, cleanse your deck with whatever technique you prefer. When I receive a new deck, I use a dried herb bundle to smoke clear any and all residual energy attachments. Energy attachments can be from the place it was sourced, to any and all exchange of hands it wound up in before landing on your doorstep. It releases your deck from unnecessary clutter. Say a mantra or prayer to begin establishing the foundations of your relationship. Here's a simple prayer:

May these cards bless me with wisdom, clarity, honesty,
comfort, and truth. I ask for the energy of love to permeate
these cards always, to care for me and anyone who these
images touch. May all visions and messages be brought
forward to support the highest good of all.

The following is a simple tarot spread to get to know a new tarot deck in which you are approaching it as a conversation with your deck. Shuffle as many times as feels needed, then cut your deck and draw five cards in the following positions:

One: The deck's personality and best qualities or characteristics.
Two: The deck's strengths as a wisdom bringer.
Three: "What areas of life do you excel at providing wisdom?"
Four: "What you are here to teach me?"
Five: "What do you want me to know to best work with you?"

When you have a brand new deck, it's nice to work more exclusively with it at first. It's sort of like getting a puppy or kitten—you pour more of your focus and attention into it to train it how to work with you and how it will best respond to you. Every tarot deck is different, and it's fine if you need a little more of your energy to establish a link. I find that my favorite decks rise to the surface when they are easy to connect with. If they are complex or not aesthetically pleasing to me, they wind up collecting dust on my shelf or go in the donate pile to my psychic development students.

A simple daily one-card draw for the first week or two of handling a new deck is sufficient. This is a quick practice to train your eye to grow accustomed to the images in the tarot. Open a fresh page in your journal in the morning. Reflect on your card for the day. Write down what comes to your mind and intuition about that card. Note what it makes you think about, that may surface during your day. In the evening, write down key events that occurred throughout the day, and how the wisdom in the card was useful.

CHAPTER TEN

Questions for the Tarot

As with any metaphysical tool, there are best practices to ensure success. Tarot philosophies among tarot readers are vast and varied, but the one that is fairly universal is that it matters how you ask questions.

When asking questions of your deck, it is best to assume 100 percent responsibility for your life choices. A question tossed out in a flurry or in a state of panic may not produce the result you are looking for. A question posed to the tarot from a centered, calm, and grounded space will produce a much more clear answer than a question put out in a state of anxiousness or anxiety. When our minds, hearts, and bodies are relaxed, we can more easily decipher the messages. It's similar to being upset about something and someone says to "calm down." It's not helpful or effective because when we are in a state of upset, we aren't thinking particularly clearly—we are reacting. So when we draw tarot cards to try to receive guidance, it can be extremely difficult to take in the insights.

As a tarot reader, I discovered rather early on that the cards would pierce my foggy confused mind with incredible clarity. There wasn't a way to "hide" or pretend with the tarot. It inevitably repeatedly showed me more of what I needed to know rather than what I secretly wished to see. For this reason, early in my tarot practice, I knew that I needed to be ready to see and learn the truth about the issues I was asking about. Taking great care around the question is one way to ensure a softer landing with the results.

Use meditation to center inside the questions you are wishing to ask. Often the first question that pops into our minds isn't really the question—it's something deeper. Try this brief meditation technique to know whether or not the question you are asking needs adjustment.

Refine and Reframe Your Tarot Questions

To start, write down a question you would like to ask the tarot. Take some deep breaths and clear your mind (I like to visualize a white room inside my mind with an exit door; when I direct the thoughts out of the room, I open space and clear the clutter of my mind). Continue breathing and relaxing into the space. Sink your awareness down into your heart center. Open your heart by visualizing waves of light gently surging through and expanding the center of your chest. It can feel so good to open your heart. You are surrounded by protection and your heart is safe to open.

From this openhearted space, bring the question again to your mind. Listen to your heart and intuition now to discover if something about the question may need adjusting. In this state, the nature of your own perceptions can deepen, as you understand much more about what's really in your hearts, not just what's in your minds.

There are a few rules of thumb that can greatly assist in reading cards for the best outcome. You may ask open-ended questions. Tarot is not the best tool for asking yes or no questions, so I advise writing any question exactly as you are feeling it in the moment and then make needed adjustments. The images in the cards reveal obstacles or tell stories about what you are feeling or thinking. They act as a magnifying glass on your subconscious telling you what's hidden from view.

Keep questions focused on the present moment. Using tarot for divination is an advanced tarot technique best explored when you have grown accustomed to understanding what the cards are telling you about your life and situation in the moment. Reading future outcomes is a delicate and rather fragile practice, and it is changeable. If you decide to read about what will happen, realize that what you are seeing is likely a probably outcome if nothing in the moment were to change.

Be willing to take complete ownership of the situation. Sometimes it is true there is little control we have over the circumstances in our lives. Using tarot to take away our own sense of agency is disempowering. Realize that in many situations of our lives, we are running the show and we hold the power to steer the course, and control our own reactions to the events and outcomes.

Here are some example comparisons of commonly asked questions and how to reframe them for the best results:

Q: "Will I get the job I applied for?"
Reframe 1: "What can I do to advance my career path?"
Reframe 2: "What do I need to know about the job I just applied for?"

Q: "Will my relationship ever get better?"
Reframe 1: "How can I improve my relationship?"
Reframe 2: "What do I need to know about my relationship?"

Q: "Will I ever be happy?"

Reframe 1: "What steps can I take to experience more joy in my life?"

Reframe 2: "What is holding me back from feeling happiness?"

Q: "What is my purpose?"

Reframe 1: "What can I do to add more meaning to my life?"

Reframe 2: "What personal skills and talents am I not using?"

Meditation, Tarot, and Spirit Communication

Combine meditation and tarot to connect with spirit loved ones crossed over. This is especially good if you feel the presence of your loved ones but don't hear clear messages from them. With these two practices you can have an ongoing conversation. Be sure to document your conversation for future reference, as sometimes their wisdom or guidance can actually be about future events.

Do a brief grounding meditation to clear your own energy, tether to your body, and prepare you to connect with spirit. Close your eyes and connect with your breath. Imagine two grounding cords of light attached to the bottoms of each foot that tether you to the center of the earth. Breathe, and release down your grounding cords any unnecessary energy in the form of cluttered thoughts, aches and pains, and anything that no longer serves you. Next, pull your grounding cords up through the base of your spine to the top of your head, where the light of your grounding cords merges and falls down around you cascading down in a field of protection.

Next, prepare your tarot deck. While shuffling, hold in your heart and mind whom you would like to connect with through the cards. Maybe there is one, or perhaps there is more than one. You can invite whomever is available. Close your eyes again, and when you sense the presence of a spirit loved one or ones, you can begin drawing cards.

The first card you lay down is in the position of, "Who is this I am speaking to?" The second card position is, "What is it you would like me to know right now?" The third card position is, "How can we best communicate in the future?"

Study the cards and journal to record the results. Before ending, breathe and release down your grounding cords any lingering energy. Thank the spirit or spirits for coming forward, and gently yet firmly ask them to go back to the light. You can invite any spirit allies/guides to assist with this process.

CHAPTER ELEVEN

Navigating the Journey of the Major Arcana with Meditation

The major arcana represents archetypal qualities or patterns of behavior that exist within our psyches. Each of us may express those patterns of behavior, because they are deemed universally human qualities. What we express depends on the circumstances we are navigating in our lives at the moment we draw the cards. In her groundbreaking book *Archetypes: A Beginner's Guide to Your Inner-net,* author and spirituality expert Caroline Myss writes, "Archetypes provide the foundation for your personality, drives, feelings, beliefs, motivations, and actions."

When getting acquainted with the major arcana archetypes, spend time wondering about a time in your past when you may have exhibited the qualities or behaviors represented by each card. For example, can you recall a time in your life where you took a risk or acted impulsively to accomplish a goal? This behavior is represented by the Fool tarot card. If you've ever had an abrupt change or something shocking or surprising happen whether good or bad, you can connect easily to the Tower card. Recalling times when you felt mentally unstable or stifled by a situation in relationships or work where you felt there was no escape is the story of the Devil card. When you needed to make a decision alone and be decisive and assertive, you were channeling the Emperor. We have all been in circumstances where we had no choice but to completely let go of control and allow things to work themselves out, a meaning mirrored through the Hanged Man.

You may be familiar with these more common archetypes: the Virgin, the Maiden, the Crone, the Queen, the Coward, the Bully, the Hero, the Jester, the Sage, the Feminine, the Masculine, the Tyrant, the Lover, the Sadist, the Rebel, the Storyteller—there are more than 325 identified archetypes. Every personality system, such as the Enneagram, Greek gods and goddesses, and yes, even astrology have throughout history sought to characterize universal qualities we may exhibit. All archetypes have a light or more positive expression as well as a shadow or more negative expression.

Because tarot is a psychological tool that works to reveal to us what may be hidden in our unconscious mind, it is highly valuable to thoroughly understand the first twenty-two major arcana cards as archetypes. You may find parts of yourself in each of them, as they exhibit different aspects of who we are, making them tremendous allies and teachers. You will ultimately find them appearing throughout your tarot readings at different times as your life changes and as you evolve and grow. We don't associate with only one archetype; the major arcana that you draw will reveal to you your thoughts, desires, feelings, behaviors, or qualities that can be helpful to you during a particular moment in time. While the court cards are also archetypes, they more often represent someone else in your life who is influencing the issue in question; we will explore their qualities in chapter 17.

The great myths that we shape throughout our lives are inherently represented in the storytelling of the twenty-two archetypes. They are pivotal milestones or turning points, which is why they are more prominent in a reading. Getting to know yourself reflectively through the archetypes in tarot is a powerful exercise for learning the cards and self-awareness.

Tarot Archetypes Key

0. Fool = Child, Innocent, Gambler

I. Magician = Alchemist, Wizard

II. High Priestess = Mystic, Psychic, Oracle

III. Empress = Mother, Giver, Nurturer

IV. Emperor = Father, Leader, Boss

V. Hierophant = Mentor, Holy One, Rule Keeper

VI. Lovers = Lover, Partner, Mirror

VII. Chariot = Warrior, Competitor, Hero

VIII. Strength = Heroine, Protector

IX. Hermit = Wisdom Bearer, Introvert, Sage

X. Wheel of Fortune = The Optimist, The Shaman

XI. Justice = Activist, Judge, Peacemaker

XII. Hanged Man = Seeker, Prophet, Sorcerer

XIII. Death = Transformer, Change Agent, Catalyst

XIV. Temperance = Mediator, Advocate, Healer

XV. Devil = Addict, Oppressor, Abuser

XVI. Tower = Annihilator, Destroyer

XVII. Star = Dreamer, Idealist

XVIII. Moon = Maiden, Divine Feminine, Crone

XIX. Sun = Divine Masculine, Creator

XX. Judgement = Messenger, Harbinger

XXI. The World = Master, Integrator

Archetypes aren't people—they are behaviors and qualities that over time can be changed through healing and the power of will. Don't concern yourself if you draw major arcana cards you don't like. All cards manifest in both positive in negative ways. So if there's something you don't like about the archetypes you've drawn, explore ways in which you can get the most out of that card, based on your current life path. For example, I really don't like drawing the Fool; at this point in my life, I'm really not looking to take many more risks or embark on daring adventures. I prefer to feel more like the Empress or the High Priestess, the loving wisdom bringers. I love to assist and support my family and the world through my spiritual gifts and compassion, insight, and love. The Fool instead advocates that I open up to something new or different. It urges me to take a chance and not to be afraid to explore a new idea, project, or venture. It can also simply advise a new approach that I've been resistant to. A shift of thought patterns or behavior can often move us through the rather dark and stormy weather of our lives.

Becoming comfortable with how the behaviors and characteristics of the archetypes can empower you in developing your own life myth, and strengthen your character.

The Fool

Keywords: Inspiration, risk, change, naïve, innocence, new
  beginnings, optimism, faith, hope

Astrological sign: Aquarius

Element: Air

Planet: Uranus

Quality: Fixed

Symbolism and Meaning

In the Fool card from the *Everyday Witch Tarot*, the cat replaces the
dog of the Waite-Smith deck as the wise, calm, and patient accom-
plice. It sits on their broom with them, knowing it would rather
go along for the risk and adventure than be left behind. Familiars
in Witchcraft are animal beings who walk through all of the magical doorways with us. They serve as profound guides and allies.

The witch is in a posture of victory, excitement, and willingness to take a leap, not knowing where they will land. They have their trusty broom, and birds swirling seem to suggest just the appropriate conditions for the witch to take flight.

The traditional interpretation of the Fool is that of a beggar or vagabond, who carries only what they need on their back, and has no other apparent responsibilities or obligations, who is free to roam the world. It is the first card of the Major Arcana, and so by the nature of its placement indicates a new journey or new beginning. There is also an undertone of innocence, as if this person hasn't had much experience and may or may not realize the consequences of their willingness to leap into the unknown. In tarot readings, this is a card that can bring tremendous hope and energy, as it can give the reader motivation to take a leap of faith, or move into a new direction of life. Change isn't always easy, but who doesn't love a chance to begin again?

This is not the time to belabor a well-thought out plan. Abandon your procrastination mode and instead realize you will only see results by moving forward and taking action. You are being urged to take a leap into the unknown, and stay future focused, particularly with an area of your life. An element of risk could be involved, and you can and should trust the process now. There is nothing that serves you in stalling your life out of irrational fear. There are times in life when an impulsive choice can shift everything for the better—this is one of those moments. This is not the time to belabor a well-thought out plan. Get out of procrastination mode and instead realize you will only see results by moving forward and taking action. You are being urged to take a leap into the unknown and stay future focused in a particular area of your life. An element of risk could be involved, and you can and should trust the process now. There is nothing that serves you in stalling your life out of irrational fear.

Meditation

When you are ready to take a breath with the Fool card, find a quiet space where you can focus on yourself for a few moments. Set up your ritual tools, and manage your environment by dimming lights and closing or opening windows. Play some gentle music. Arrange your body so that you are in a comfortable position, one that allows you to breathe deeply and stay grounded.

Close your eyes if it's comfortable for you. You may find keeping your eyes open more comfortable, in which case allow your gaze to settle on a point or object in front of you.

Begin by taking several long, slow, deep breaths in and out.

When you feel your body and mind moving into a soft and receptive space, it is time to try accessing your natural well of courage and confidence. Sense or feel the next steps of your path opening from a space of an endless, wondrous possibility. Allow it fill you like a warm, glowing light. Notice where you feel that warmth settling into your body, where it feels brightest. Nurture that glow and let it build and expand within you.

When you feel this realm of inner courage flowing, allow its brilliant light to spill out all around you, becoming a bright beacon. Bring your attention back to your breath now, and enjoy surfacing feelings of newfound determination and bravery. Embrace the sensations of feeling fearless. You are courage embodied. Imagine the light now overflowing, engulfing the space you are in.

Imagine now what it would feel like to take that first step toward your goal, to begin making purposeful movement toward the future that you want. Feel the certainty of your conviction as you witness yourself opening new doors, as the path ahead pulls you toward it. Notice how it feels to hold your intention and action together, becoming integrated now, merging and becoming like one.

Notice how your body feels holding space for this new direction. Focus on your breathing again. Breathe in focus, intention, desire, and joy. Breathe out any lingering doubts, anxieties, or fears that this is not possible. Say out loud, "I am worthy of my dreams. I am enough. I am strong and capable. I am ready to move forward with my dream."

Slowly and gently open your eyes. Give yourself a few additional moments to reflect in a journaling exercise.

Journal Prompt

Take a moment to reflect on what the Fool card means to you right now. Answer the following questions in your tarot journal:

1. What new beginnings are you considering at the moment?
2. How is the idea of beginning something new impacting you emotionally?
3. How do you typically respond when faced with change?
4. Is there anything you need to make the leap feel safe?
5. List three to five new things you would like to try.

The Magician

Keywords: Manifestation, alchemy, skills, talents, resourceful-
ness, action, willpower, concentration
Astrological sign: Gemini
Element: Air
Planet: Mercury
Quality: Mutable

Symbolism and Meaning

Throughout movies, television, myth, and folklore, Crones are
typically portrayed as isolated, eccentric, ugly old witches. This
interpretation has merely distracted us from the potency and
power they truly hold. Here we can see Crone energy as a powerful force, similar to the more traditional archetype of the Magician. In the image, the Crone is nearing the final stages of their

own life. Setting caution aside, they are in a state of pure creation, using the talents and skills built up for a lifetime. Others fear their power, though the truth is they are only able to manifest the most beneficial healing for themselves and humanity. This important wisdom-keeper, midwife, and healer manipulates the energies and forces of nature and of the universe for the good of the world. They beckon us not to fear their powers. Staying on their good side, we can sense they will loyally assist us on our life path and with our own healing.

The more traditional interpretation of the Magician includes the ability to manifest desires, wishes, and dreams. The Magician is a highly skilled alchemist, capable of creating something out of nothing. There is desire, willpower, and the desire to transform. The saying "as above, so below" is steeped in the imagery in the Waite-Smith Magician card. When drawn, this card reminds us we are a micro version of the universe, and are capable of creating tremendous things. It is generally a positive card to receive in a tarot reading. If anything is out of balance, the Magician actively seeks to restore it. Another archetype that applies to this card is the Sorcerer.

You are capable of manifesting from a place of centered mindfulness at this time. Take care what you put out into the world in the form of thoughts, words, intentions, and prayers, as they have untold consequences. Spend time pondering what you want to release from life and what you want more of. Keep your spiritual practices strong and motivated by positive outcomes, and the greater good of humanity. Be clear what it is you are open to attracting into your world right now. Direct your willpower in ways that heal, help, and support rather than simply destroy. Know that opportunities will soon replace whatever is falling away from your life. Use your innovation prowess and imagination to harness new directions and positive outcomes. This card suggests a delicate and powerful moment in time that is best served by a balanced, careful approach. Wish no ill will toward others. Give of your natural gifts and magical abilities freely and it will return to you tenfold.

Meditation

Sit comfortably, close your eyes and begin to take a few slow, deep inhalations and exhalations. Bring to mind something you have longed for and desired to manifest in your life.

Next, begin to notice any limiting or negative thoughts. Wander into those thoughts and ponder on the recurring themes and how these thoughts have impacted you in the past. Ask your higher self to help you see the ways in which you are holding yourself at a distance from having what you desire. Start by bringing one major pattern to mind. Notice all the different times in your life this theme has been present. What was happening in your life at that time? What type of environment were you in?

If there are circumstances and logistical barriers to having what it is you desire, breathe deeply, and ask your higher self what you can do to lift the barriers around pursuing those dreams or goals.

Now, with the intention of clearing out old wounds and beliefs from the past that have magnetized this energy to you, it's time to let go of what isn't serving you.

Imagine being surrounded by a flood of healing energy from spirit, source, or the Universe and ask that it fill you up and heal you up from the inside.

When this energy fills you, invite a visual representation of the patterns, beliefs, or thoughts you are ready to dissolve. Flow this healing energy directly from your heart center to this representation and as that it also be healed.

When you are filled with this healing energy, invite forward a visual representation of the person, belief, or pattern that you are ready to dissolve. Imagine flowing this healing energy from your heart to this other being or situation and asking that it, too, be healed.

Now turn your awareness to what you would like to manifest. Fill yourself with feelings of completion and joy as if it has already happened, and allow yourself to imagine all the details surrounding this accomplishment.

Take a few more breaths. Send a stream of energized thoughts and feelings you have gathered to this image, desire, or dream in addition to deep gratitude for being a part of your life.

Journal Prompt

What are three things you can do to take steps today towards your desired wish, dream, or goal?

The High Priestess

Keywords: Psychic insights, sacred knowledge, intuition, emotion, spiritual wisdom, inner voice, spiritual mentor

Astrological sign: Cancer

Element: Water

Planet: Moon

Quality: Cardinal

Symbolism and Meaning

The High Priestess of the *Mermaid Tarot* stands at their altar, the wind whipping at their cape, their focus unmoved by the crashing waves. This card amplifies the element of water, making the ocean the focal point. We have no choice but to be drawn into the watery image as the moon overhead adds a level of drama and intensity to the situation. Water represents intuition and our psychic abilities, and the moon our inner most selves. Our emotions move like the water, at times overwhelming like waves crashing down upon us, and at other times cleansing us of our pain through tears. We can know the truth and find a path forward when we engage our sixth sense and trust the guidance of spiritual wisdom.

This ancient seer and healer holds a tremendous responsibility: healing, giving insights, and revealing the truth to all who cross their path. In the Waite-Smith deck, the High Priestess sits on the throne of wisdom, waiting for those seeking their insights and knowledge. The High Priestess was seen as someone who held powerful esoteric wisdom and who had access to the messages available to us from beings that exist in between worlds; a holder of important spiritual truths, and a seer, a healer for the weary soul. Time spent with the High Priestess was restorative. With wisdom gained, there would be no further insecurities or doubts about which path to take, their piercing gaze permeating the depths of our soul, becoming a powerhouse of revelation.

Step back from a situation and reflect, dig deeply into your own intuition, and listen to your inner voice. It is time to surface your own High Priestess wisdom. The spiritual wisdom that lives within you is surfacing now, and it's important to slow down so you can hear it. You see more than you realize, and the truth will surface over time. A spiritual mentor may cross your path at this time, or someone who can assist you in gaining the clarity you crave. Nothing is really as it seems—there are potent forces at play behind the scenes, and more can be understood by reflecting on esoteric or spiritual wisdom. Don't be afraid of the depth of emotion you may be feeling; it is your inner compass and guide. Don't forget to give back to the High Priestess in the form of a prayer or mantra, or an acknowledgment in a space of deep gratitude for

the phenomenal well of wisdom available to us all. Giving gratitude maintains balance and keeps the connection with the spiritual forces working with us alive.

Meditation

Use this simple third eye activation to connect more deeply with
your own inner voice, inner knowing, or inner vision.

Prepare by finding a comfortable spot to sit, preferably on
a chair or the floor where you can sit while lifting your spine
upright. Your posture will assist in opening your channel, supporting your third eye and chakras.

For a rotation of ten breaths, focus all of your concentration on your breath, in through your nose, and out through your
mouth. You can practice this rotation until you are comfortable
with it. Watch with eyes closed your breath flow in and out naturally, with each inhale and exhale. Allow this to establish a rhythmic breathing pattern. You may choose to repeat a simple mantra
in your mind such as "relax," "let go," or "release."

As you pay extra attention to the gaps in your breath, watch
your thoughts carefully. If your mind should begin to wander,
bring it back by observing your breath.

Shift your attention to your third eye, which is located right
between your eyebrows and just about a quarter-inch back, in the
position of your pineal gland. Lift your internal gaze to this location. Try not to strain, just rest your gaze there with a gentle and
consistent focus. Now imagine the energy of your third eye beginning to rotate like a small orb of purple light. As you focus on this
orb, it begins to expand.

Continue to repeat the mantra you chose. You may begin to
feel a tingling sensation or a heat or pressure around your third
eye and forehead. This is a wonderful sign that your inner eye is

opening to allow your own inner guidance to surface. Continue this practice for five to ten minutes.

Journal Prompt

What did you experience during the meditation for the High Priestess? What sorts of insights, images, feelings, impressions, thoughts, or messages did you receive? How can you continue to honor your own inner guidance on a regular basis?

The Empress

Keywords: Divine Mother, Gaia, love, birth, regeneration,
sensuality, creativity, nurturing, abundance

Astrological sign: Libra

Element: Air

Planet: Venus

Quality: Cardinal

Symbolism and Meaning

Instead of a scepter or wand, the Empress is holding the conch shell,
a symbol of fertility. The shell is also blown to help purify the environment from all harmful effects, as she is the great protector of the
earth. When you hear its call, the Empress is actively averting natural
disasters and assisting all living beings. They blow it to get your attention and spark action, and also to banish evil spirits from this world.

The standard meaning of the Empress is one of unconditional love for all of humanity. They are the epitome of kindness, transmitting nurturing and comfort to all who cross their path. They exude a loving wisdom that makes all feel welcome, accepted, and loved for who they are. The Empress also reminds us of the importance of loving oneself. They urge us to get in touch with our own sensuality, so as to bring more pleasure and joy into our lives. The Empress signals fertility, and when this card is drawn, the traditional message is to enjoy the abundance of the harvest. As the archetype of the Mother, the Empress seems to beckon to us to care for and nurture ourselves and others.

For a moment, whatever is causing you strife or suffering is buffered by the overwhelming sense that in the arms of the Empress, everything is going to be okay. They open up a deep well of compassion and understanding and even agree to assist you in healing from your pain. The love envelopes you in a blanket of comfort. Whatever you have been going through, it's important to prioritize your own self-care. Invite the nurturing support of those around you, and see to the well-being of others with healthy boundaries intact. You may be called to help and assist others at this time; be careful not to give so much of yourself you forget about yourself in the process. Fertility is about new beginnings, and the Empress has come to help you birth something new! They govern sensual pleasures and spark the chemistry of sexual attraction. They seek to rejuvenate and make things whole. They are the ever-present, loving, and fierce protector of the natural world.

Meditation

Use this meditation to connect to the power of mother earth, or Gaia. This is who the Empress best represents and is a wonderful way to connect to the wisdom of this card.

Sit in a chair, on the floor, or at the base of a tree. Take a few deep, relaxing breaths and center yourself in the space, grounding yourself in your body. Imagine a beautiful bright white chord of light attached at the base of your spine at your tailbone. That chord stretches downward, extending like an elastic band of light all the way to the center of the earth. Allow several breath rotations as you deepen your connection to the center.

As you breathe, imagine that chord becoming a tunnel of light that you are now traveling down. With each breath, transport yourself deeper and deeper into the center. As you get closer to the earth, you feel a pulse of deep love, calm, and compassion. You feel the embrace of the earth surrounding you now, cradling you in a space of comfort. Touch the soul of the earth, and allow yourself to rest deep into this space of healing and respite.

When you are ready, imagine bringing the energy of the soul of the earth back with you through the tunnel. Allow this healing and comforting energy pulsate throughout your entire body beginning with your feet, calves, legs, up through your hips and torso, up through the top of your head.

As you emerge from the soul of the earth, you have brought its healing energies with you. Feel this energy nourishing you, healing you, and anchoring in your heart center. Thank the earth for this chance to connect, merge, and heal. In connecting deeply with the earth, you have also connected deeper with the gifts of the Empress and what she invokes within us to heal.

Journal Prompt

What did it feel like to travel to the center of the earth? Could you sense, feel, and imagine the earth's nurturing embrace? What tidbits of wisdom did you bring back with you?

The Emperor

Keywords: Stability, leadership, authority, focus, discipline, willpower

Astrological sign: Aries

Element: Fire

Planet: Mars

Quality: Cardinal

Symbolism and Meaning

In the *Dark Wood Tarot*, the Emperor is represented by the ram, a symbol for the zodiac sign Aries. Aries represents the pioneering, edgy, unconquerable, unstoppable sides of us. Aries is the fiery zodiac sign of pure willpower in motion. No one has the opportunity to dominate us when the ram appears. This animal initiates through bold and courageous determination. Feeling invincible, this creature breaks down all the barriers before it without flinching. Blazing trails, the ram may go where no one else has ever gone before.

The standard meaning of the Emperor is one who is in authority in a current situation. This person recognizes full responsibility to dictate the action steps for an entire kingdom, and they do so willingly and without complaint. There is utter devotion to the cause at hand, and they will not hesitate to strike down whoever or whatever is in their path. The traditional Emperor calls the shots; makes all the decisions; and is grounded, calm, cool and collected in doing so. No matter who or what would bring disorder into our lives, the Emperor is untouched by the chaos, with a razor sharp vision and decisive action. This tarot card advises that we act rather assertively to achieve our goals or to solve a problem. The weight and responsibility is on our shoulders.

Use the energy of the ram fully in your current life situation. Take charge and begin to see a possibility with concrete action steps you can take. Whatever current situation you are facing requires firm, assertive, and authoritative decisions. You are no longer waiting on the sidelines for an issue or situation to resolve itself. You are ready to face any challenge with courage and conviction. If you are leaning into the support of an authority figure who has come into your life, also represented by the Emperor, you can trust that soul is here to help you overcome this situation and make strong choices. This is a pivotal time in your life that requires confident action.

Meditation

This meditation can assist you in connecting to the assertive, wise guidance of the Emperor. It is helpful to have a journal or notebook ready to jot down what you receive after the meditation is complete.

Imagine in your mind's eye you enter a great hallway of a large beautiful and rather ancient stone building. As you wander through the hallway, take in the images, colors, or feelings of being in this place. Notice what artwork graces the walls, gaze up at the ceiling, the vast expanse of this space beckoning you further down the hallway.

Feel the depth and complexity of this place. Many have been here before, also on an important mission to receive direction and guidance. You inch your way closer to the place within, where you'll be met by a wise guide and visionary. Eager to meet them now you turn the corner into a large comfortable and bright room. At the far side near the window is a large mirror.

Walk up to the mirror now. Gaze into it as the image of a being begins to materialize, staring back at you. This image stirs courage and hope within you, as it appears to be ready and confident about what you have come here for.

Invite assistance in the form of thoughts or questions for the image gazing back at you. Notice any feelings, thoughts, or symbols that appear, as well as words or messages that come to you, even if it is only a stronger boost of courage to move forward with something important.

Journal Prompt

How did it feel to be in that large ancient place, walking along the grand hallway to meet up with your own wise inner leader? What did that wise master look like, feel like, or how did it appear to you? What guidance did you receive, and what can you do to continuously access the confidence you felt to act on that guidance?

The Hierophant

Keywords: Holy wisdom, education, sacred, knowledge, beliefs, spirituality, conformity

Astrological sign: Taurus

Element: Earth

Planet: Venus

Quality: Fixed

Symbolism and Meaning

The *Everyday Witch Tarot* modernizes the character of the Hierophant, represented here as a yoga master before whom two yoga students are engaged in a yoga pose. Certainly yoga is one way to reach the sort of spiritual wisdom the Hierophant resembles. The teacher is simply guiding them to it for themselves. They are all wearing striped stockings, a whimsical throwback to the witch in the film *The Wizard of Oz*. This "holy" or "sacred" master represents that wisdom in our lives that can turn us towards a calmer, more centered pathway. Sometimes we are the ones who have steered ourselves off course. Living a spiritually centered life takes discipline and constant attention. The Hierophant is that sacred belief system, methodology, or ideology by which to live. Luckily there are many paths to choose from and try out.

The Waite-Smith Hierophant traditionally means adhering to traditional or religious norms. There are structures within society that are already established, constructs that are already in place and have stood the test of time. This card surfaces in order to test you to discover whether it is best to accept those constructs and structures rather than going outside of them to invent your own. It is typically seen as a strong voice of guidance on the side of conformity, rather than individuality of thought and expression. There may be times it is simply not acceptable to conform, and the Hierophant ignites the deep inner questioning required to come to terms with our own values and beliefs. This card is where convention meets the unconventional, the traditional meets the nontraditional, and the individual meets the conformist. You must decide where you stand on that spectrum in the face of this wise guide.

Your life is cluttered with a mass of activity and responsibilities at this time. It may be leaving you feeling strained, stretched out, and depleted. It is time to find the balance of body/mind/ soul. It is time to explore what can truly help you in unlocking your own spiritual freedom from within. This may be in the form of a retreat, a class, a book, a podcast, or your inner voice. Dig deep and access your own inner authority, your own inner belief systems, reconstruct what is not working for you, and reinvent the rules you operate by if needed. This will cultivate a renewed sense of peace, understanding, and self-acceptance. You can make room for your soul to breathe and expand in the spaces you share with the Hierophant. Feeling the lost pieces of yourself being returned, or reviving something that felt asleep or dormant, you are once again made whole. You suddenly sense you are being submersed in a holy wisdom, enveloped in spiritual truths, cleansed of worldly concerns, and touched by the heart of the universe. You begin once again building in a source of spiritual resiliency each and every time we go to this sacred source. The Hierophant exists in many places and in many forms; when we thirst for renewal, we can always find it.

Meditation

Journey to meet an important holy one and helper on your life path like the Hierophant. This is a moment to pause and to ask a question for spiritual insight.

After connecting with your breath and finding a centered, relaxed flow within, close your eyes and connect with your inner vision.

Imagine, sense, or feel yourself wandering through a sacred sanctuary, perhaps a wooded resting spot by a stream or a beautiful enclosed garden. Allow this sanctuary to be a space only for you—a space to rest, relax, and recharge.

Continue gently breathing, and wander through your sanctuary. You feel as if you have been guided here and now open your senses to the scents, visions, feelings, and tactile sensations of this place.

You wander to an inner chamber and walk through to meet a wise master or ally. This wise master holds important esoteric knowledge. You ask for guidance and insight regarding a particular question or area of your life. As you sit quietly, you open your inner ear to the wisdom being provided you now. Spend a few moments here, and when complete, slowly return to the room and write what you received.

Journal Prompt

What was the question you asked this wise master? What impressions, thoughts, or messages did you receive? What is one thing you might do with what you discovered?

The Lovers

Keywords: Balance, unity, love, relationships, choices
Astrological sign: Gemini
Element: Air
Planet: Mercury
Quality: Mutable

Symbolism and Meaning

The mirror is a reflection tool. In this card it represents the idea that we don't need to look beyond ourselves to discover and subsequently know who we truly are. Swimming in the beautiful yet sometimes turbulent seas of life, we suddenly encounter moments when we see our true self and our true nature. It can be a startling realization and immensely gratifying to meet new sides of ourselves, and the best part is that we get to do this our entire lives, multiple times throughout the course of one lifetime if we are lucky. Knowing our true self affords us the chance to build strong and lasting relationships, as those we bring into our world can then act as complements to our own gifts, skills, and talents. We are better served for the time we take in self-realization, gazing into the mirror of our own psyche, discovering ways to balance and uphold who we are from a deep space of inner resolve.

In the traditional Lovers tarot card is the story of Adam and Eve from the Bible. In its purest form, this story is about our own personal awakening to seeing who we really are, coming out of innocence and knowing the depths of our own fears, desires, and impulses. It is about the blending of the two sides of each of us, our conscious and subconscious selves. In the beginning, our conscious and subconscious were harmonized and unified. After the fall, however, they separated, causing a spiritual death and a separation from God. The more accessible interpretation of this card is about partnership, romance, and love. It is more practical to use this card as a way to reach penetrating awareness about our own hidden desires and wishes, and the even give and take of needs and expectations in relationship. It can be about our own relationship with ourselves, and the battle we engage with in our own minds, where ego takes the reins and we neglect our true selves. Discovering who we are restores and honors both sides of us. From this space we are whole.

The ultimate experience of loneliness resides in not knowing the self. Spending time in isolation with the intent to discover your own true nature is one of the greatest gifts you can give yourself and your relationships right now. It is through that space of deep inner reflection you can ignite your own passion for yourself; eventually, a lust for living and being who you are in the world will develop. This is the moment to evaluate relationships and part-nerships of all kind, whether with yourself or with others. If you are questioning a romantic relationship, there's no better place to begin than in the mirror. Is there something that you need to take a hard look at within the built in subconscious patterns, habits, or barriers you have erected in your own relationships? Your relation-ships need evaluating.

Meditation

This is a sitting or reclining meditation that will assist you in open-ing your heart center. When we live with an open heart, more can be known and understood about our own relationships both with others and ourselves.

Adjust your body to achieve a comfortable pose, either sitting or lying down.

Once in place, take time to sink into your breath. Feel the ten-sion and trapped energy in your body release as you breathe and relax. Engage in eight to ten rotations of deep breaths, each one relaxing you more than the one before.

Shift your focus now to your heart center. Hold your attention there, and feel the slight sensations of your heartbeat. With each breath, engage the pulsing sensations of your heart and invite waves of energy to move through you. With each breath, each heartbeat opens your heart further and wider.

Feel how with each breath, you find a deeper sense of ease and a peace. Now bring to mind something or someone that you love to mind. Allow that feeling of love to grow. Notice how won-derful it feels to focus on something that brings you immediately into feelings of love.

Now imagine sending your own pure stream of love outward to your inner circle, your family, your neighborhood, your community and to the world. Notice if you feel hesitant or fearful about allowing your heart to expand. Pause and wonder what might be present that would stop you from feeling free to let your heart's energy flow.

Journal Prompt

How did it feel to open your heart's energy? Bring to mind a challenging relationship, whether with yourself or another. What insight now do you have coming from an openhearted space about those relationships?

The Chariot

Keywords: Decision, control, certainty, courage, action
Astrological sign: Cancer
Element: Water
Planet: Moon
Quality: Cardinal

Symbolism and Meaning

In the *Everyday Witch Tarot*, the character is driving a motorcycle, the ultimate symbol of travel and movement instead of a chariot. This choice amplifies the adventurous tone of this card. Their expression is one of surprise, perhaps realizing they have arrived at a definite crossroads on their journey. This crossroads has been coming toward them for some time, and it may not be the only time they have been in this conundrum. Not knowing where to go next is the internal dilemma. However, we see clearly there is absolutely no more aimless wandering now; they must choose one direction or another. The sphinxes are replaced by street signs pointing This Way and That Way. Perhaps divine guidance will choose the way.

In the Waite-Smith deck, the Chariot is about using your own strength and power to overcome obstacles. The charioteer has a competitive spirit and someone who is willing to charge ahead in spite of what might appear to be an insurmountable journey. This card traditionally speaks to the inner will and the blind confidence to pursue a path not knowing how it will end. It showcases what it means to take charge and also remain reined in so as not to throw off the balance. Regardless, there is a charging forward into life with assertiveness and willpower. It is up to you to steer the horses in the right direction. No one else can do it for you.

The time has finally come to make a choice. You have been on a long journey, and the gateway of possibility is now open to you. No matter how fast you have been going in your life, it seems as if there is no amount of speed could make this choice for you. Make things final and move in a direction that opens up to certain possibilities you hadn't considered. The moment you are firm and decisive will clarify the next steps, and not a moment before. You may still be feeling uncertain, and that's okay. Remember, there are no right or wrong paths in this scenario. However, staying in the midst of uncertainty means you do not get to move forward. Staying still is a choice, and in this particular situation it doesn't help you—it hinders you. There may be a part of you that knew all along the best path to take, it was just difficult to admit to it. You are the only one truly in control of your own destiny.

Meditation

This meditation connects you to the feeling of movement required to take the reins of the Chariot for yourself and steer the course.

While seated in a chair, take a moment to place both feet on the floor. Connect with your breath. Steady your posture. Relax into the chair. Center yourself in your own mind, and imagine gently clearing anything that may be residual energy around your third eye, like dusting out a small closet. Envision the cobwebs being swept away, opening and sharpening your inner vision.

Now you are taking the reins of your own chariot. With confidence, step into it. As you take up the reins, feel the tension in your hands and arms as the horses bristle, waiting for you to signal that it is time to move forward.

Consider the destination you wish to reach. It may be a personal or spiritual destination or it may be relational or even vocational. You may be ready to pursue a passion that has laid dormant. Commit to moving in that direction. Signal now to the horses that it is time to go.

Feel the excitement and energy that moving towards a destination provides you in this moment. Feel the air rush over your skin, the sun in the sky, the elements now rising up to meet you. You resolve to continue no matter the obstacles, no matter the weather. Notice what surfaces around you: doubt, fear, whatever the real or perceived barriers are, and watch as you race furiously past them. One by one, the obstacles fall away.

You begin to see the destination now in your own inner vision. It is no longer a far-off pipe dream or wish. As you visualize it, you push aside any remaining trepidation, accepting that you have made it—you have successfully overcome the barriers and are ready to meet your goal head on.

Journal Prompt

How did it feel to take the reins and sense yourself moving toward the destination of your dreams and goals? What barriers or obstacles did you see yourself moving through? What is one thing you can do now to remove the limits to your success?

Strength

Keywords: Courage, inner power, perseverance, resilience,
   bravery

Astrological sign: Leo

Element: Fire

Planet: Sun

Quality: Fixed

Symbolism and Meaning

I am particularly struck by the incredible symmetry in this card; it
is balanced and centered. The blooming rose emerging from the
stone wall suggests the power of will inherent in all life. We, too,
have an innate strength and willpower available to us. The character sits pensively and passively, clearly holding the power here
while hypnotizing the snake. The color red indicates passion and

power, and we see symbols in their upper chakras supporting clarity and vision, steadiness and confidence. We don't always know what sources of willpower and resiliency we have access to until we are in the moment where it is needed. In moments of crisis, even we can depend upon our own inner strength reserves, and this card reminds us of that truth. We are more resilient than we may realize.

In the Waite-Smith deck, Strength's traditional meaning is about stamina and persistence, knowing you have what you need to overcome any obstacle. There is strength not only of will, but also self-composure. The character in the card is stroking a lion, the symbol of what is wild and out of control in your life. You are patient, capable of achieving what you set your mind to because you do not succumb to perceived or irrational fears. You know that with calm and attentive action, your steady and persistent choices will get you where you need to go. This card traditionally lends a stabilizing force from within; when drawn, the message is that you can rest in your own deep well of inner strength. I have traditionally seen this card represent the built-in capabilities and willpower to attain certain outcomes. Drawing from our own strength builds character, and also the stamina to overcome whatever else might stand in our way.

Something in your life is testing your ability to remain emotionally balanced. If you've been emotionally triggered or are undergoing turmoil or a crisis, you may be feeling like you may lose your temper at any moment. In those moments, you could do or say something you would come to regret. It is therefore wise to contain and channel the fire within, the burning rage surfacing at this time before it explodes. Face your fears, and do not be afraid to access the fortitude you need to move forward, in spite of the circumstances. Find meaningful and healthy ways to use your big emotional energy for good. You can make a difference! Strength summons your own inner warrior, your own inner courage. You may find now is the time to lead a situation towards a strong conclusion that works for all involved. It is well within reach, trust your abilities to source it.

Meditation

This meditation is a reflection exercise for building up your own inner courage, reassurance, and self-recognition of times in your past when you overcame fear and chose strength.

Take a moment to breathe and center yourself in the moment. Find a pleasant space, perhaps a room with sunlight beaming through the windows, or in a space surrounded by nature. Choose the most pleasant meditation space. One that makes you feel welcome, calm, and at peace.

As you continue to take breaths in through your nose and out through your mouth, center yourself in your body and the environment. Breathe deep down into your belly, and allow any residual tension in your body to melt away with each successive breath. Soften your forehead, jaw, and tongue. Allow your belly and hips to relax and soften.

Move your body from side to side, continuing to breathe and release until you feel any remaining tension dissipate.

Wander back in time to a memory where you recall being faced with an obstacle or a barrier that seemed at the time insurmountable. This was a moment in your life when you chose strength over fear and were able to overcome the obstacles you faced.

Put yourself back in the moment when you made the decision to remove the barriers and what happened next. Recall any doubts you may have had about moving forward, and also recall how it felt when you succeeded in spite of what was attempting to stop you. Draw forward the feelings of accomplishment. Remember the tenacity and courage it took to stay the course.

Consider an area of your life now that may require that same courage, tenacity, and strength. Imagine facing the fear and digging deep to access any creative energy or willpower that can assist you at this time. Allow the force of that energy to drive your enthusiasm. You can do this!

Journal Prompt

Rewrite the experience from your past including as many details as you possibly can, where you overcame obstacles to achieving your goal. What can you replicate from that time and bring forward to your current life path? How might it help your current life path to access your own inner courage and strength? List all the areas of your life in which you wish to apply your renewed sense of strength and personal power.

The Hermit

Keywords: Rest, relax, regenerate, insight, contemplation, soul searching

Astrological sign: Virgo

Element: Earth

Planet: Mercury

Quality: Mutable

Symbolism and Meaning

In the *Everyday Witch Tarot*, the Hermit is using the fire as a light source, beacon, and guide instead of a lantern. Witches often use fire ritually as a tool for purifying and sending their own thoughts, spells, and powers of intention into the universe. Fire provides the energy and force behind our greatest intentions and also our worst acts as humans. Witches use this for magical purposes. When we are before a fire, it commands utter respect, as we fully honor its fierceness and unforgiving heat. We know the danger it holds, and yet we can't deny the hypnotizing focus it can bring our own practices. It ultimately assists as a divination tool to seeing our way more clearly. A beautiful symbol of wisdom, the owl in the tree reminds us of what is possible when we take time for inner reflection. Being in nature (in this case, in the woods) and near some of the most benevolent and wise living beings, including trees, can bring us to our own inner guide.

According to most standard tarot decks, the Hermit is the mountaintop sage, the one who has acquired a wealth of spiritual knowledge to share with others. Inside the lantern of the Waite-Smith deck is the six-pointed star known as the Seal of Solomon, a symbol of wisdom. He also carries a staff, a symbol that in those days represented the authority and power that comes along with having attained such intelligence. Guiding themselves through the darkness of night that represents unanswered questions and conundrums, they finally reach the pinnacle of awareness and knowledge. We too sometimes have that same task—to go within, face our own dark night of the soul, and come out of it knowing more about ourselves and our lives than before. There are times we travel alone, and the Hermit accurately represents these times.

The events of your life have pushed you to the limit, and now is the chance to go within. Take time to retreat, rest, relax, regroup, and regenerate. It is time to allow your own inner guidance take center stage. You have met your limit attempting to understand what's expected of you from society. At times you have felt like a cog in a machine. There are times for engaging in the rhythms of society and conforming to those unwritten rules. There are also times when it becomes necessary to know the self outside of what others say is right or wrong, which isn't about disregarding societal constructs as much as it is about cultivating a rich inner world and allowing our own inner truths to strike us with their piercing clarity. This moment is calling for the escape to your inner realm that will ultimately make you stronger and more confident in the choices you make in the outer realms.

Meditation

In this guided meditation, connect with the ever-present light source that exists within you.

In a comfortable space, settle into a rhythmic breathing pattern that slows down your mind and thoughts, bringing you fully into the present. For a moment, take in the hectic pace of your life. Through the eyes of honesty, become aware of anything that feels heavy or burdensome.

See yourself standing before a mountain. Gather your determination, and begin trekking up to the pinnacle. As you walk, you turn to look back periodically to take in the vast expanse and landscape around you. Breathe now, and imagine this vastness around you. This place feels familiar. It is a replica of the expansiveness of your soul, your inner world, and it is a representation of the space you create for yourself to go within. Allow this to grow and flourish as you imagine yourself climbing higher and higher up the mountain.

As you draw closer to the pinnacle of the mountaintop, you see or sense a beautiful bright light drawing you in. It feels so warm and welcoming, you are compelled to continue your assent, your curiosity drawing you closer.

Inside the light is deep awareness and peace. Allow this light to draw you safely within and feel its glowing power engulf you in an inner knowing that all is well. Remain in the glow of the lantern until you feel complete.

Slowly descend the mountain now, releasing any need to over-analyze what you received. Bask in the shiny new insights. Allow their warmth to comfort you.

Journal Prompt

How did it feel to reach the pinnacle of the mountaintop of your own soul? What did you discover there?

The Wheel of Fortune

Keywords: Cycles, changes, destiny, luck, good fortune
Astrological sign: Sagittarius
Element: Fire
Planet: Jupiter
Quality: Mutable

Symbolism and Meaning

The playful attitude and posture of the witch in the Wheel of Fortune from the *Everyday Witch Tarot* shows them standing next to a prize wheel. The symbols on the wheel reveal the multitude of possibilities open to us at any time. We instantly feel an inner tension, as there are several options on the wheel and they are all great. As in life, often we cannot have everything all at once, and this witch looks at us with hand on hip taunting us, which will we choose? The witch's attitude and stance begs the question: Do we ultimately choose our own destiny, or is it all up to the spin of the wheel? More traditional tarot meanings for the Wheel of Fortune include the philosophy that there are times in our lives we must allow things to unfold and take care of themselves, that sometimes we are not in control and greater forces are at play, and that there is a universal design involved. This way of thinking can often be reassuring, and in certain instances reminds us how very little control we generally have over the major life phases and changes in our lives. A giant wheel is embedded with alchemical symbols, the elements, and on the outer corners are creatures that represent the four fixed signs of the zodiac. The letters spell ROTA (Latin for wheel) and backwards TORA (shortened version of *torah*, meaning "law"). The general tone is that of hope and optimism, as if everything may work out in our favor. When we are open to the signs and symbols all around us, things can fall into place through synchronicity. Nevertheless, it indicates a significant turning point, that we can be assured.

What in your life is now ready to begin a new chapter? There are seasons to our lives, times when we must simply let go and allow the turning of the page. This is one of those times. Take time to honor what has led you to this point. Reflect, marvel at the past, and grieve what is now ending, so you can achieve a full release into the future beckoning you. This is a chance for a new beginning! Whether it's a career change, marriage, a new baby, becoming an empty nester, or going back to school, you are ready for the events to unfold, creating the next chapter of the book of your life. You may be feeling that something is shifting but you don't yet know what; don't worry, it will be shown to you soon.

Meditation

Take a few moments to find a comfortable place to rest and unwind from your day. Get comfortable.

Close your eyes and begin to tune in to your breath, inhaling through your nose, exhaling through your mouth. Tune in to the sensation of your breath. Feel your belly expand, and allow your body to soften as you exhale. Don't try to change or force anything. Become aware of where the breath fills you up and the path it takes as it leaves you.

Feel the breath just above your belly; guide, don't force the breath. Gently guide the sensation into this space. Inhaling cleansing light, and exhaling to continue softening into the space around you.

Quietly or out loud, say to yourself:

"I ride the waves of change."

"In motion I am comfortable."

"In chaos I am confident."

"I arrive home to myself."

Continue to repeat these words as a mantra for a cycle of nine times. Breathe, deepen, and release yourself into the truth of the words as this meditation brings the words deeper into your consciousness. Feel your mind shifting to include them as your new reality, governing any upcoming changes, chaos, or turmoil the Wheel of Fortune may bring.

Bring your awareness back into the space now. One final deep breath. You are still. You are confident. You arrive home to yourself.

Journal Prompt

What was it like to feel those truths reverberate through your body? Did you feel any resistance? If so, where? How can you use that awareness to heal?

Justice

Keywords: Accountability, consequences, law, truth, injustice, cause and consequence

Astrological sign: Libra

Element: Air

Planet: Venus

Quality: Cardinal

Symbolism and Meaning

This card isn't about legal trouble, though sometimes it can be. It is more about recognizing that no matter how much we lie to ourselves and tell ourselves everything is okay, causing harm to others is likely to come back to us in the form of mental anguish, guilt, shame, or devastating loss. If we've given back and contributed positively in some way to the lives of others and society, that is also bound to come back to us in the form of blessings or good fortune. Justice sees and knows everything, as the half blindfold suggests. The black and white kittens fighting with one another drive the symbolism deeper that there is no middle ground to be found, it is one or the other, left or right, up or down. The law book on their lap reminds us that universal laws are what they are, and nothing we say or do can change them.

The Waite-Smith deck shows a judge holding the balance scales, as we wait for the consequences of our actions to be determined. If we've been operating from a morally and ethically sound space, we will see the results of our good actions. If our actions have caused harm, whether intentional or not, we may realize the consequence through unexpected, even painful outcomes. This card reminds us it is not too late to do what's right. When drawn, this card definitely urges us to carefully examine the choices we are making, asking if we are sure that we are willing to face the consequences or the outcomes of those choices. Reflecting on what is truly right and wrong, there is no in between with the Justice card—the decision is black and white, one or the other.

You may be feeling unsteady and uncertain regarding an important decision right now. It is good to slow down rather than act impulsively. Consider whether or not you are prepared to accept the outcome of your own actions. The right option will show things that positively affect the whole. If an option may be harmful, hurtful, or destructive, it may be wise to pause and re-evaluate before moving forward. Engaging your intuition can be helpful, because it will alert you to the possibility of something potentially going wrong. Or, you may be wondering why it is that things are suddenly turning in your favor. This may be the karmic reward for your own good deeds, decisions, and choices. Self-awareness and self-honesty are critical components right now. Examine potential situations in which the course of action you took or are about to take could be unjust and find ways to take responsibility, hold yourself accountable, and seek to make things right.

Meditation

Justice is an omen for the coming need to make an important decision. Justice insists on carefully examining right from wrong, and to make a choice that does not waver in the face of uncertainty. There is no gray area with Justice. Use this brief meditation exercise to help you with a major decision where you are concerned about the consequences. Some decisions are difficult because they challenge us to choose the more ethically sound path forward.

We all make bad decisions at one time or another but can learn from them; they don't need to reverberate into our future. On a pad of paper or journal, write down something you would consider a bad decision in your past. You know now it was a bad decision because it was either regretful or negatively affected your life in some way.

Now set your writing aside and close your eyes, settling comfortably into the space. Allow a rhythmic breathing pattern to be established. Remind yourself that you are safe. This exercise will empower you and help you break old patterns. Reflect upon what caused you to make that bad decision or decisions.

Chances are it was a decision made out of childhood conditioning or familiarity, fear, or panic. Begin to feel yourself letting that decision and the consequences be released now. Feel self-forgiveness surfacing now. You can let those things go now with this mindful meditation.

What do you want and need now? What decision are you trying to make? Can you feel or sense the consequences of making that decision? Take this time to really let your mind unwind and feel the clarity surfacing on what the right path forward is. This decision doesn't need to be stressful. Let this exercise bring peace of mind, and certainty to your own process.

Now bring to mind a decision you made where the consequences positively affected your life and the lives of others. Repeat the meditation steps, going through the process. How did this have a positive impact on your life? What happened inside you that allowed you to come to the conclusion, and how did it feel when you pursued that choice? What was the outcome?

Notice the different sensations in your body now. Where do your decision-making powers live and vibrate within? Now come back slowly to the moment, ready to reflect and write the two different choices and experiences. Take your time; there is no need to rush this reflection.

Journal Prompt

Document all the different feelings, thoughts, and sensations that surfaced during this meditation and with the two different decision scenarios. What did you learn about your decision-making prowess? What do you need to do to step forward confident of the decisions you are making now?

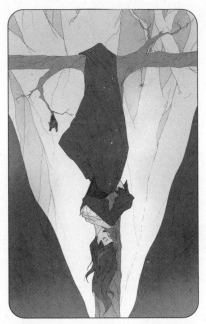

The Hanged Man

Keywords: Surrender, sacrifice, letting go, indecision, missed
   opportunity
Astrological sign: Pisces
Element: Water
Planet: Neptune
Quality: Mutable

Symbolism and Meaning

The more supernatural features of the Hanged Man from the *Dark Wood Tarot* suggests the power that certain unseen forces can have a tremendous impact on our fate. Representing immortality, a vampire contentedly hangs in the balance between the upper and lower worlds sleeping while the bat's piercing red eyes watch over things. The tone of the symbols suggests a restful wait for something, perhaps for forces from beyond to intervene and resolve the situation. There is a sense that certain life events must be left to take their own natural course.

The more traditional version of the Hanged Man shows someone with a halo around their head hanging upside down bearing a serene expression, as if fully accepting their fate. This enlightened act of surrender suggests martyrdom for the greater good. Seeing the world from a new perspective, even upside-down, can lend insights not previously known. The original interpretations suggest a time when it is more appropriate to wait things out than to take action, as well as the need to pause in order to see the best way forward. Going about life from the exact same patterns often leads to the same outcome, sometimes there is a need to completely shift perspective and see something in a new way. At times it is best to surrender a perceived sense of control in the life situation.

Something new is emerging. When you stop to see it more clearly, it can lead to a stronger and more definite outcome. It is wise to periodically take a moment to stop and assess where things are in life and if any course correction is indeed needed. Consider putting important projects on temporary hold to see if things are in fact going in the right direction. Taking time away from your routine can help you see things in a new light. If you continue to resist or push forward, there are bound to be obstacles along the way. The Hanged Man gives you permission to take a deep breath and hit the pause button on life. It will serve you well for the long term. If you are feeling stuck or restricted by something in your life right now, it might be helpful to evaluate what might be holding you back right now. Lightening expectations and changing up your routine may help you shift your energy so you can move more freely.

Meditation

We often draw the Hanged Man card when we are waiting for something to happen. There is often a sense that we cannot rush things. The situation needs our pause, forced or unforced. For some, that pause can feel deeply uncomfortable. Use this meditation on the Hanged Man to guide you to a slower, more relaxed zone of inner calm. May it remind you that nothing must be done right now—and that includes you.

This is also a wonderful meditation for bringing a pause to moments when you might be overwhelmed by the events in our chaotic world right now. We cannot sort out our place and purpose when we are triggered by strong emotion. Through the space of letting go, we can find our center spot to create a positive space for effective rather than reactionary choices.

Begin by adjusting your sitting position. If you are on a chair, be sure your feet are on the floor. If you are on the floor, try sitting cross-legged, and gently place your hands in your lap, right hand over the left hand, palms up, your right index finger gently touching your left thumb. This position is called the "peace position" and is right in harmony with the vibe of the Hanged Man.

Gently close your eyes and try sitting with a smile on your face. Take a deep breath, inhaling and exhaling a few times. Breathe in deeply until you feel the air reach down into your abdomen, expanding and contracting with each breath in and out. Breathe out all of your worries, stress, and tension.

With the vehicle of your breath, let everything go, all of your responsibilities. Let your mind embrace a relaxed and peaceful vibe free from worry. Allow every muscle in your body to relax, from the top of your head to the tips of your toes.

Feel a sense of lightness beginning to enter your body and mind. Think joyful and cheerful thoughts. Imagine you are sitting alone in a vast, open space full of your idea of peacefulness.

Focus your mind on the center of your body around your abdomen. Imagine your breath as delicate as a bird's feather landing in your belly, so delicate, so soft, so light. Imagine a blue orb of light settling into that space in your body, expanding that sense of peacefulness wider and wider. Remain here as long as you wish, continuing to expand that sense of peacefulness.

When you have reached this deep state of relaxation, mind calm and feeling still, share thoughts of kindness, good wishes, and peace out into the world. Imagine this sphere of love and good wishes expanding in all directions from your body's center toward the world.

Journal Prompt

Make a brief list of things popping into your mind you can release for now, let go of, or pause until you feel more steady, grounded, and centered to proceed.

Death

Keywords: Ending, transformation, rebirth, change,
transition
Astrological sign: Scorpio
Element: Water
Planet: Pluto
Quality: Fixed

Symbolism and Meaning

Death in the *Dark Wood Tarot* holds an hourglass, a reminder that
time has run out. The figure also holds a scythe, a bleak reminder
that Death comes for us all in the end. Death has the final say, and
yet we know that through Death is always rebirth. Death is only
the end of the prior form of something. Transformation through

destruction brings a new beginning, what rises from the ashes is more pure. The angel in the foreground looks defeated, knowing they have no choice but to surrender. The child gazes up with innocence, representing the naïve attitudes we sometimes have in life, deluding ourselves that nothing will ever change.

The rather ominous tone of the traditional Waite-Smith Death card is filled with an ominous darkness and is typically an omen of unwanted change. The skeleton or angel of death rides in on a white horse, the ultimate symbol for freedom. This card reveals an intense and apocalyptic scene. The imagery is grounded in the resurrection story from the Bible, as we see a holy figure in the backdrop, praying over the dead. How we respond to major changes in our lives is of the utmost importance. Will we heed the call to a new beginning or allow the grim reaper to force our hand, destroying everything?

Whether it is a loss or a major change of some kind such as the end of a relationship, a career path change, or significant spiritual shift, Death in any form is exacting and merciless. The best course of action right now is to let go and move through any grief or discomfort this time in your life may bring. Let Death bring you through any adversity you are currently facing in your life. Where you are hesitant to let go, you can call upon the gift of the scythe to cut what is not needed and give you courage and resilience to continue. This card isn't about literal death; instead it is about a new adventure that awaits you—you are freed from the previous form of your life circumstances. The terrain may be unknown, but wisdom suggests things are working in some sort of divine order. All is as it should be. Trust that you will survive whatever transformative processes are surging through your life will bring you to the other side even stronger and more alive.

Meditation

As the saying goes, the one thing in life we can be certain about is change. Death illustrates this, often appearing when we are on the brink of an ending, leading to a new beginning. Use this meditation to settle more easily into the changes in your life.

Quick reminder: It works best to use this particular meditation when you are feeling grounded and stable of mind. When emotionally triggered, it can be difficult to use mindfulness appropriately.

Sit comfortably with your eyes closed. Connect with your breath and move the air in and out of your lungs with ease. With each breath, settle into your body. Relax your belly and release any tension from your day.

In your mind's eye, see yourself standing on the edge of a cliff overlooking a vast valley. You don't know how, but you know deep down inside your soul that you were somehow led here, to this moment. Allow your gaze to wander across the horizon and take in the beauty all around you. The light touches your skin, the breeze blows over you, and you feel the stirrings of something brand new just over the ledge.

You turn around in an effort to see if you can go back. It looks dark and dreary behind you, and no matter how much you want to go to the beginning and start over, or return things to how they were, deep down you know it is time for this change to happen.

As you glance over the ledge, suddenly you see protective and beautiful beings of light rising up to greet you. They will support you now, and are beckoning you to take the leap, the one that takes you to the next step or phase of your life. It initially feels scary but you gather up your courage and step into the great unknown. You instantly feel the support of those protective and loving beings guiding you.

There is a sudden feeling of freedom and release from a past situation that was no longer working for you. You get the sense that things are going to be more than okay—as a matter of fact, they are going to be great! You just needed the push to make the change and to take the leap into the vast unknown ahead of you.

Take a few breaths and slowly come back into your body and into the space.

Journal Prompt

What did it feel like to take the leap into the unknown knowing there were supportive beings waiting there to guide you?

Temperance

Keywords: Moderation, peace, balance, calm, serenity
Astrological sign: Sagittarius
Element: Fire
Planet: Jupiter
Quality: Mutable

Symbolism and Meaning

Conch shells in the *Mermaid Tarot* replace the cups of the Waite-Smith tarot. In this image, an alchemist carefully and patiently puts together a potion or an elixir, having gathered the precise mixture of cosmic energies to create the perfect mixture for what's next in your life. In this moment it's okay to surrender your path to Temperance. The way forward is through calculated and moderate action steps. The halo around the mermaid's head signifies a divine connection as well as the forces of the eclipsed sun and moon working together with intensity and intention. We get the feeling Temperance is gathering universal energies to use for good. The Mer-folk are mystical teachers and guides, so we get the sense here that it's all going to be okay and that we can give in and allow universal forces to guide us.

Standard meanings of Temperance include slowing down the pace of movement and motion in your plans. The word "temperance" itself means "moderation." Sometimes a gentler, calmer approach is what gets us further in life than a robotically manipulated, controlled, and seemingly well-plotted design. It can be hard to wait for things, but with Temperance, there really is no choice but to give in to the natural flow and cycles of nature—there is a magical space available to us when we collaborate with the forces of the universe. Temperance gently reminds us we have done what we can, this is now time to hold steadfast to our center, remain calm and focused, and trust in the cosmic forces of the universe to guide us forward. There is a cosmically balanced tone to Temperance that is to be honored and trusted.

Whenever your life is calling for balance, and a calm, calculated pathway forward, you will draw Temperance. This card is asking you to avoid impulsiveness in your decision making while also reminding you that everything falls into place in due time and sometimes requires you to relinquish control. This is not the moment to force or push things. You are in danger of making things much more difficult than they need to be. A path of ease sometimes requires slowing down to understand what is missing. You have been through a lot, and to force the issue is to potentially set yourself up for grief, disappointment, or crisis. Seeking reprieve to allow the dust to settle after a hard journey is exactly the right action.

Meditation

Use this meditation when you feel the business of life overwhelming you. When you crave a slower pace and take in your surroundings with more contemplation, harness the inspiration of Temperance through this moment of stillness.

This meditation requires a pause somewhere in nature. Depending on where you live and what outdoors access you have, find a calm and serene location to spend a few moments in silence. Do not worry if you live in a busy urban environment far from the woods or a lake or a river. Locate the nearest public park. Oftentimes sacred spaces such as libraries, museums, and churches have space outdoors around their buildings for you to use.

Once you are there, you may proceed with this observational meditation. It is also helpful to turn off your phone so you won't hear or feel a notification. Our lives are so hurried that just a few steps to reduce the access others have to us can be so relieving in themselves.

Find a spot to sit where your body will be comfortable for about ten to fifteen minutes. Take a few nice deep cleansing breaths, and allow your eyes to scan the surroundings you are in.

Now let your gaze land on the first thing you see, e.g., a tree, the grass, leaves, the snow, a bird, etc. Stare at that object for several minutes just breathing and relaxing into the moment. Notice the shape of it. Take in the color. Does this object move? If so, allow yourself to follow it with your eyes and observe without distraction. What else are you noticing now? Be deliberate when you change your focus, only going to one object or creature at a time. Study the pattern in the tree trunk or pick up a leaf and trace the lines running through it or its shape.

Continue to move your eyes now to the next object around you in nature. Something as simple as a rock or a pinecone can be an object of intense study. Wonder about how those objects came to be. There is life happening all around you. Think about the lives of objects or beings in nature.

Now take in the air around you. Feel the air coming into your lungs in a big, deep breath. Observe all the life in nature happening around you without your control or influence. Imagine your own life right now; the world is ever-moving around you, and yet you are not a part of it. You can take a moment anytime you want to stop the train of your life. It's okay to stop, slow down, and rest in the now.

Journal Prompt

How does your body feel after doing this meditation? What impact did it have on your senses? On your mind?

The Devil

Keywords: Limitation, fear, ego, barriers, sabotage, addiction
Astrological sign: Capricorn
Element: Earth
Planet: Saturn
Quality: Cardinal

Symbolism and Meaning

What looms over us can be so daunting that we feel as if we have no choice but to submit to its demands. The person standing in the foreground of the Devil in the *Dark Wood Tarot* has a sword in hand, ready to confront the monster, who has a club in one hand, ready to beat down and punish anyone about to cross their path. In the monster's other hand are chains, fully prepared to remind us of the sometimes overwhelming captive power of our darkest fears, the things that trap us and keep us small. At best, the Devil represents the bullies of the world, those who tell us we can't do it. This card can also represent our own inner negative self-talk, the tapes that play in our minds telling us we aren't good enough. Or, it could represent anyone who loves to see us suffer and struggle.

The Devil card from the Waite-Smith deck traditionally signifies limitation, neglect, and the dark sides of us, especially in our relationships. When we refuse to deal with the shortcomings and toxic patterns in our relationships and ourselves, something typically happens to shift the course for us, forcing us to face our own inner demons and darkness. When we don't deal with those things, we become chained to the part of our psyche that tell us we don't deserve happiness, contentment, or love. Avoidance can drive us deeper into depression, addiction, and escapism, sometimes making a mockery out of our desires and needs. The opportunity lies in an inability to openly process, face our fears, grapple with our darkness, and heal. Some equate this card with the concept of purgatory or limbo, a holding space that truly keeps us captive without the ability to be free. Until we are willing to face the truth and deal with it, the evil one looms over us, our hearts, and our minds, feeding us toxic messages and untruths.

This moment requires extra diligence as you face your own barriers, whether they are mental, spiritual, or relational. Something is threatening your own ability to achieve a sense of fulfillment in your life. It's time to pause and examine what you are telling yourself about your current circumstances that may be untrue. Avoid playing the martyr or the victim and take a more active role in solving the problems plaguing you at the moment. It is sometimes easy to blame the world and everyone in it for what we have in fact created for ourselves. Have you played a hand in feeling bogged down and suffocated? Avoid self-destructive behaviors, especially those that jeopardize your health or mental wellness. Examine your own habits under a microscope until you see more clearly the role you may have played in arriving in this situation. It might be a good time to seek spiritual guidance or traditional counseling to see beyond the brick wall of limits that seem to continue stacking up. You may have been a part of getting to this point, but with some self-forgiveness and plenty of guidance, you can create a strategy and long-term solutions to your dilemma. It can be difficult to see under the influence of the Devil.

Meditation

This is a great meditation for freeing the mind, especially when you feel trapped in your mind or are spiraling into negative patterns of thought. When you gain mastery over the ability to manage your thinking mind, you set yourself free.

This meditation can easily be done either sitting or lying down. The most important thing is to have plenty of time to allow this process; you don't want to be rushed.

Take a few minutes to center and ground yourself. With your eyes closed, imagine that you have a large golden cord of energy attached at your tailbone, at the base of your spine. This energy cord stretches like an elastic band all the way down to the center of the earth. The earth's center is a tremendous recycling plant for energies and a powerful ally and helper for us to release energy and heal.

With each breath out, imagine releasing any energy held within you that is no longer serving you. Breathe in and gather up all of the negative energy, tension, and stress. Breathe out and release all of that energy down your grounding chord. Feel the sensations of deep and tremendous release.

Now go to the room in your mind with your own inner vision. Notice all of the thoughts wandering in and out of that room. Pay attention to thoughts that seem kind, and then notice thoughts that may be unkind or antagonizing you persistently and stubbornly clinging to the interior of this room.

You begin to understand and realize how often your thoughts take over and control you. Now is the time to get acquainted with those thoughts, negotiating with them to change or demanding that they exit the room of your mind. Take a few minutes now to attempt to negotiate with your thoughts, inviting them to soften, telling them what you want to be thinking instead, giving them a chance to cooperate, change course, or leave.

Any thoughts that are willing to compromise are allowed to remain. They are gentle with you, and you with them. They are quiet and undemanding of your attention. They feed you energy and contribute to your sense of well-being.

Now you can feel, sense, or see which thoughts are resisting your attempts to change them. They are simply not allowed to stay. Firmly direct them to the exit door, and once they are out of the room of your mind, close and secure the door so they are no longer allowed back in. Ponder how it feels to have only the most cooperative thoughts hanging out with you. Relax into this moment of mental peace, and give yourself as long as you wish to just be.

You have done an amazing job! You have singlehandedly taken control of your own thoughts. When you find your mind running amok again in the future, come back to this exercise. Our thoughts can often be our own worst enemies, and we don't need to allow those thoughts to overpower us.

Journal Prompt

Was it challenging to get unwanted thoughts to leave the room of your mind? What was your experience of being in the room with only the most helpful, cooperative, and kind thoughts? In what areas of your life do you feel you might be able to use this meditation?

The Tower

Keywords: Upheaval, destruction, turmoil, change, endings, empowerment
Astrological sign: Aries
Element: Fire
Planet: Mars
Quality: Cardinal

Symbolism and Meaning

In the Tower card from the *Everyday Witch Tarot*, the witch is sheepishly gazing back at us with a grin as they examine the destruction at the hand of their magic wand. Their familiar, a cat, peeks out from under the bushes, and we definitely get the sly feeling of self-satisfaction from them both. It is done; there is no other choice but to clean up the rubble and start again. We don't need to wait for things in our lives to end. We can do the blowing up ourselves, which often creates a clean slate upon which we can build something new. There is often something much more magical on the other side of the destruction, as it makes room for new beginnings.

More traditional tarot decks interpret the Tower as a moment of unpredictable and sudden turmoil and abrupt change such as a job loss, forced career change, location change, eviction, separation or divorce, financial disaster, or a need to begin again and build from the ground up. Whatever we build on a firm foundation such as strong ethical and morals can stand. When we build something on a weak foundation such as greed, selfishness, or ego, it cannot stand for long and will at some point fall. When we build something for impure reasons, the satisfaction doesn't last long and brings about the need for more.

Whatever is happening in your life, now is not the moment to climb under the covers and ignore it all. Where you are feeling the tug of an existential crisis, the Tower generally commands swift and sometimes abrupt changes in the areas of life affected by any turmoil. When this card surfaces, there is little question about what needs a complete overhaul. You know what it is, and if you are feeling trepidation or fear, you may wish to call in your spiritual guides, friends, and community to support you. You also may be feeling the powers of magic at your fingertips—everything you touch begins to transform before your eyes. Quick change is exhilarating to some and debilitating to others, but the thing the Tower does not typically do well with is procrastination. If you stall an impending change or resist or ignore it, the shift may happen anyway in a way you didn't want. Use your magical gifts to take action, and face into whatever is presently challenging you.

The area of life it affects may be internal rather that external; if no outer circumstances must change, take a look inward.

Meditation

This meditation exercise is wonderful for bringing a greater sense of stability and security to your life, something the Tower is a master at disrupting.

Let's begin with grounding. Gently move your attention to the bottom of your feet and place them on the floor. Take a moment to rest your attention there. Feel the rootedness your feet feel resting on the floor or ground. Feel the foundation holding you, supporting the rest of your body.

Now gently move your attention to your breath. Take a relaxed breath, moving the air in and out of your body in slow waves. Just be with your breath and your body, your feet, and the ground. Allow the breath to wash over and through you now. No need to control it, just allow the fluidity of your breathing stabilize and center you.

As you breathe, remind yourself in this moment that even your breaths change; no two are alike. This is breath. Just like a wave, wild and free, just like the impermanence of life that at times takes hold of us and whips us through unpredictable changes.

When you take your next breath, feel the air coming into your lungs. As you soak up the air, imagine the waves it brings through your body. When you let your breath go, notice how it feels to empty your body and prepare for the next breath. We let go of our breath unconsciously all day long. This is a great metaphor for life and the moments we need to let go of. Come back to the rootedness of your feet and the ground underneath. Notice that even with the constant change of your breath, the moving in and the moving out and releasing, you are still rooted in your feet and the ground. Grounding is always available to us, reminding us that we are held amid the changes in our lives from moment to moment.

Journal Prompt

Make a brief list of things you know you can do right now to bring yourself a stronger sense of control and security amidst the changes the Tower ignites. What is one thing you need to bring some peace to the hectic nature of the changes in your life?

The Star

Keywords: Inspiration, faith, hope, healing, rejuvenation
Astrological sign: Aquarius
Element: Air
Planet: Uranus
Quality: Fixed

Symbolism and Meaning

We can immediately see the power in the wishes blown into the conch shell in the Star card from the *Mermaid Tarot*. The secret or inner dreams and desires float through space, and we see that energy becoming connected and integrated with the cosmos. It's possible they aren't only sending up wishes and dreams for themselves but for others as well. Water meets sky in a tremendous blending of emotion, sensitivity, and passion merging with the heavens. There is a delightful balance here between the water and sky as the foam rises up, messages of hope and desire. It seems that with every motion of their body, more energy around them begins to build and gravitate towards them in a swirl of potential and possibility. Whatever energies are being gathered, it appears to be happening effortlessly.

Practical and spiritual abilities combine in the original Waite-Smith card interpretation. This card brings messages of hope and renewed power to carry on with life. When this card surfaces in a reading, the traditional meaning is that we have made it past a long and arduous journey, one perhaps ridden with complication or struggle. In the process, we have discovered our own resilience and courage. There is deep gratitude to be felt as we reconnect with our own sense of inner peace that things are happening in divine order. It is time to rid ourselves of any limiting beliefs. In addition, stars are traditionally a symbol of our ability to connect with something greater than ourselves, the bigger picture, the part we play within an expanded universe. The well of our inner-most urges and needs doesn't run dry, it just changes over time. We can connect with that space in the moment and clarify what those needs or dreams are.

You have overcome a long and difficult journey. What has transpired in your recent past is no longer a part of your present or future. You have a clearing now, a blank slate upon which to dream, wish for, create, and manifest what is possible. The universe hears your call and is working closely with you to sculpt your dreams into something real. This is a time of significant personal growth. You are entering a calm and peaceful phase of your life; the difficulties are over now. Transforming from the old to the new you requires faith in the process and releasing any fears blocking your own inner vision and intuition.

Meditation

The Star surfaces often when we have achieved a major milestone or overcome a major obstacle. The vibration of gratitude harmonizes your thoughts with the positive things happening in your life. It is a wonderful reflection. Gratitude puts us in the mindful space of what is going right in our life versys what is not.

Use this meditation to promote feelings of deep thankfulness for spiritual, physical, and emotional wellbeing. A mantra is a repetitive saying that stimulates a peaceful, mindful attitude. You are going to repeat a gratitude mantra with all of the things you are currently grateful for. Notice how your body and mind responds to you speaking your mantras out loud.

First, find a spot that supports relaxation and is comfortable: a chair, the ground or floor, or a bed. Take a moment to center yourself. Turn off devices that may disrupt you. You can close the door to the room you are in and dim the lights.

Begin by taking some deep breaths through your nose, fill your lungs with air. Let your breath out through your mouth. In through your nose, out through your mouth. Settle into a smooth and relaxed pace of breathing.

Now, it's time to practice your gratitude mantra. The mantra is: "I am grateful for _____." Repeat this out loud at least ten times, naming something different with each mantra repetition. Continue with this exercise as long as moments of gratitude surface in your mind. If you are having difficulty coming up with things you are grateful for, just begin with your immediate environment and expand beyond that.

For example, "I am grateful for this comfortable spot," or "I am grateful for a body that keeps me alive." You could be thankful for the trees outside your window. Or you could be grateful for the sun, moon, and stars in our greater universe all of which contribute to life on this planet in major ways.

Journal Prompt

Write down your gratitude mantra and all the things that popped into your mind that you are grateful for. Were you surprised by what appeared?

The Moon

Keywords: Illusion, confusion, unconscious, emotion, intuition

Astrological sign: Cancer

Element: Water

Planet: Moon

Quality: Cardinal

Symbolism and Meaning

The Moon in the *Mermaid Tarot* is an incredibly active card and character. The invisible waves of energy emanating from the moon are so aptly portrayed in this card. The Moon participates in sending out just the right melody to those who are open to hearing it. Do you ever get the feeling that the moon is sharing its most vibrant, healing energy with us, especially when it's full? The symbolic waves of energy emanating from the being who represents the moon serves as a metaphor for how the moon collaborates with us. If we listen, we can hear its message of comfort and support for our lives. The moon's messages come to us through our dreams and daydreams, our heart's longings and desires, a constant and steady stream of awareness and understanding.

The Moon is the symbol of the unconscious and our dreams, revealing to us our inner emotional landscape. Traditionally, this card was interpreted as the surfacing of painful memories or emotional distress. The Moon often clouds our reality, lingering in the shadow sides of ourselves, bringing to light our deepest fears and insecurities. The dog and wolf standing in the foreground of the Waite-Smith card represents the tamed and wild parts of our psyches. Through our own unconscious unfolding, we discover more about ourselves. The Moon consistently illuminates a higher path of consciousness. This is a time to slow down and proceed with caution. This can be a time of deep uncertainty, confusion, and illusion. Not everything is as it may seem. Pay attention to what your inner voice and intuition is telling you. You may not have all the information needed to move forward. You may be experiencing the triggering of a painful memory, surfacing grief, or dealing with rising fear around a particular area of life. Sometimes at a very early age, fear becomes a part of our subconscious. As adults, we may inadvertently show this fear as fear of loss, separation, abandonment, or feelings of helplessness. This is a time for dealing with the surfacing unresolved grief, trauma, or emotional turmoil that you had no choice but to set aside. As a result, that pain became buried within your subconscious mind. Now is the time to actively address your own mental health. Journaling and meditation are spectacular tools for this, and you may decide you are ready to reach out to a therapist or spiritual guide for further counsel and support.

Meditation

This meditation exercise will help release subconscious fears and help you manage any powerful emotion that may surface at any time.

Begin by finding your center. You will sit silently during this meditation for about ten to fifteen minutes with your eyes closed. Unlike the other meditations in this chapter, this exercise is designed to surface emotions that are familiar to you. You can be anywhere to engage in this process. It is best to be in a place where you know you won't be disrupted but not mandatory.

Select an emotion, sadness, fear, anger, happiness, and so on, and begin by feeling it fully. If it helps to focus on something you associate with that particular emotion that may be helpful. Silently say to yourself, "I am (the emotion)." Fully experience what it is like to both say and feel that emotion. Stay with it until you feel it completely.

Now replace the words "I am" with the words, "I feel (the emotion)." Notice how it feels in your body to shift from "I am" to "I feel." Experience the subtle difference, including where it shows up in your body and heart, and the new relationship to the emotion.

Now shift again by saying "I am aware of feeling (the emotion)." Experience the awareness. Next shift into saying, "(The emotion) is welcome." Just feel into this openhearted awareness. Go through different emotions and repeat the exercise, simply observing how your body feels as you move through them, getting present in them.

Journal Prompt

Which emotions did you try for this meditation exercise? What feelings or thoughts did they each invoke? What messages did your body send you during this exercise?

The Sun

Keywords: Success, optimism, happiness, energy, health, vitality

Astrological sign: Leo

Element: Fire

Planet: Sun

Quality: Fixed

Symbolism and Meaning

Maiden, Mother, and Crone dance together in the middle of a sunflower field. Each of them has sitting nearby their own personal familiar, a cat. The Sun from the *Everyday Witch Tarot* is a symbol of life and growth. The sunflowers and the witches' joyous tone represent the dawn of a new day and the hope of good things to come. They three figures are barefoot and carefree, and it looks warm, lovely, and pleasant where they are. We are reminded that in addition to letting the sun to shine upon us for restoration and renewal, we must also allow our inner light to shine. Sunflowers also symbolize self-respect, authenticity, and embracing our own unique individual gifts.

The more traditional interpretation for the Sun is about coming out of the dark, radiating light, warmth, happiness, and success. No matter what area of life this card relates to, there is a tone of tremendous optimism and permission to feel good about the direction life is now taking. Embrace the joy and good feelings right now; life can change in an instant, so it's time to revel in the good vibes all around you. The card can also be a messenger telling us to notice what barriers might be preventing us from fulfilling our dreams and goals as well as how they may be removed. The enjoyment of life's many blessings is highly indicated.

If you are dealing with something challenging in your life in your recent past, drawing this card heralds a happy, satisfying, and successful time period. The areas of your life that have undergone difficulty will now experience a reprieve, and others around you will marvel at how you are handling things. You may feel full of energy and ready to complete projects. This is a time of blossoming of your inner self, bringing about the opportunity for the world to truly see you. The card is a positive omen of happy relationships, health, career, and with a deep sense of satisfaction. Do not dim your light—shine it bright!

Meditation

The Sun is a wonderful and versatile card to meditate with; there are so many options! If you love candles, you can choose a yellow, gold, or orange one to light as a symbol and representation of this card. To incorporate the outdoors, you could sit outside with the sun on your face or by a sunny window in your home.

This is the perfect "Join the Story Meditation" card (see chapter 4). When you begin this process, it is helpful to first do preliminary grounding and connecting with your breath exercises. Ground with your feet on the floor. Feel the energy of the earth rising up through the soles of your feet and coursing up through your legs, to your torso and head. Balance your breathing by taking in air through your nose and breathing out through your mouth. When you feel centered and calm, it's time to enter the story.

First, take in the image of the Sun card. Study it and commit as many of the details as possible to memory. Next, close your eyes, and imagine entering the scene of the card. Wander around this paradise in your inner vision, and allow your senses to recreate it in your imagination. Interact with your environment, then become one of the characters in the card. Notice what it feels like to become a part of this exciting yet peaceful scene.

Allow yourself to remain in the story of the card, receiving whatever insights or messages you can about your own life. Invite the Sun to share words of encouragement and inspiration with you. As the meditation comes to a close, reconnect with your breath and express gratitude for all the blessings your life holds right now.

Journal Prompt

What did it feel like to become a character in the scene of this card? What did you see, sense, feel, and notice as part of your experience?

Judgement

Keywords: Transformation, change, truth, self-awareness, awakening

Astrological sign: Scorpio

Element: Water

Planet: Pluto

Quality: Fixed

Symbolism and Meaning

The symbolism of Judgement in the *Dark Wood Tarot* is significantly different from the more traditional representation. The corpses' hands coming up from the ground suggest the urgency and pressure to complete the next steps, whatever they may be. There is no escaping the process of transformation, symbolized by the character in the card surrendering to the vampire's bite. Making the choice to immortalize, it would appear the character is entering an atmosphere of complete surrender, ready for whatever is to come, embracing their own immortality.

The story of the judgement day from many different mythologies is well represented by the traditional Waite-Smith imagery. People rise from their graves, responding to Archangel Gabriel's trumpet call. Where they will spend eternity is to be determined; they are waiting to be judged by God. Judgement invites plenty of self-evaluation and facing the truth about life circumstances. If you've had an awakening of sorts, you may be seeing things differently now. This card's traditional messages revolve around seeing things clearly and making the necessary changes needed to avoid spinning in potentially unhealthy situations. When this card appears in a spread, the weight of any decision that we need to make is usually a bit heavier. That heaviness can indicate something majorly life changing, so careful thought is advised.

What in your life might be posing as a threat to your own immortality? If you need to shed baggage that is holding you back from the learning and growth we are all capable of, now is the time to relinquish it. Judgement presses into us a sense of urgency to honestly examine what we are doing with our one precious life. It demands that we look hard at our own imprint and impact on the world. Everything is beginning to become clearer to you and should not be swept under the rug or ignored. This card represents the situation in question becoming "as good as it gets." Like reaching a pinnacle of personal success, it can also mean fulfillment or the successful merging of our inner and outer worlds.

Meditation

Judgement asks us to take a moment to apply an invisible microscope to our own lives. This inner wisdom meditation will hopefully help you take a bit of a life path inventory, seeing clearly what you have accomplished and whether or not they align with your values helps this card's assistance to shine.

This reflection meditation draws upon our inner wisdom and intuition. We spend so much of our time trying to think our way through issues and life challenges and end up ignoring our own inner voices. First, bring to mind one particular area of life you feel the need to make changes in, but aren't sure what those changes should be. Write this area down and reflect for a moment on why it is time for a change.

Now spend about ten minutes connecting to your body and breath. Slow down your body's rhythms, get centered, and clear your mind. Scan your body from head to toe, and use your breath to gently nudge any stubborn areas of tension to release. Remember to drop your shoulders. Loosen your jaw; let your tongue rest easily in your mouth. If you become distracted, just bring yourself back to your breath, your meditation anchor.

Now bring into your heart the aspect of life you would love to see change. Be still. Just breathe, and avoid trying to "think" it through, make lists for problem-solving. Instead, allow feelings, images, and thoughts to surface in your mind. When you let go of the need to cognitively problem solve, you are accessing your inner wisdom and intuition.

Remain in this still, quiet space, repeat your breathing, sink your own awareness down into your heart, and pay attention to what is surfacing. It may be a feeling, a message, a thought form, or an inner knowing. All of this is connected to your own inner wisdom. You may feel challenged by feelings of fear or self-doubt.

Stay with this meditation until you feel that anxious, fearful stirring dissipate. Instead, begin to sense the magnetic energy of possibility pulling you forward. Notice any insight that feeds you

energy and makes you feel safe, calm, energized, and motivated—
that is your own inner wisdom speaking!

Notice how it feels to take actions based on what surfaced.
If the thought of taking those actions feels bad, go back to your
breath and release all feelings of fear and doubt. You can cycle
through this exercise as many times as you need for a life area or
concern. Each time, notice how your intuition begins to pick up
new impressions and information.

Journal Prompt

What impressions, feelings, or information came to you through
this reflection meditation? What did you learn by placing one area
of life under your gentle gaze?

The World

Keywords: Wholeness, integration, achievement, fulfillment
Astrological sign: Capricorn
Element: Earth
Planet: Saturn
Quality: Cardinal

Symbolism and Meaning

The World is holding the wands, symbols of manifestation and creation, while suspended between heaven and earth. At this point on the journey, there is no need to strive any further toward a destination. You have arrived! The completion of a milestone is indeed a sweet elixir. The animals in the four corners of the card represent the four elements, and the image's earthy quality reminds us of how integral our role is in the delicate balance of all of life on this planet. You can see the profound look of accomplishment on the figure's face; they are no longer floundering, wandering, or lost. Everything is exposed, and they are unafraid of being seen. This is one of the most gratifying experiences of the human condition—to be fully seen and honored as a contributing being on this planet.

In many traditions, enlightenment or nirvana is represented in similar ways. The being in the traditional Waite-Smith card has completed this journey and then some. This card is seen as an arrival point, and themes of fulfillment and completion permeate the scene. Symbols of success and infinity, balance and evolution grace the image. There is unity and wholeness, a balance of both our inner and outer worlds; some traditions would consider this card to be associated with enlightenment. We get the sense gazing at this card that there is a delicate balance to the forces of living on this planet, and we, too, are responsible for this it.

It is definitely time to reflect on your journey to now and celebrate your accomplishments. This moment has been a long time coming and deserves acknowledgment. If you haven't quite yet achieved the moment of completion, know that the World popping up in a tarot reading reminds you that all is well in hand and you are on your way to the fulfillment of a long time goal. You are stronger and wiser than when you began this process and perhaps have revealed to yourself what you are truly capable of. It's natural to want to celebrate the triumphs, no matter how long the journey has been.

Meditation

Use this reflection meditation to track an area of your life in which you are feeling successful at the moment. Pull out the World card from whatever deck you work with, and silently gaze into it, allowing prior positive life events to begin flooding your mind.

Recall a recent time in your life when you accomplished a huge goal or completed a major milestone. Or imagine yourself successfully completing on something you have wanted to accomplish but due to circumstances haven't been able to.

Remember what it felt like when you resolved to move forward to complete this goal. What happened in your mind and heart to keep you motivated to finish it? Also bring to mind what obstacles or limits you worked through to persevere and continue pressing forward. Write down any skills or talents you incorporated to help you succeed.

If you are on the cusp of taking the leap with a huge goal, what personal traits or strengths can you apply to this process to stay the course? Reflect on what might be needed to follow through and who you may need to ask for help. The World is an amazing beacon of hope that catalyzes your own willpower and momentum toward your hopes and dreams.

Take a moment to close your eyes and imagine what it will feel like and look like to accomplish your goal. Allow your mind to show you what may be available to you should you choose to continue to move forward. Using the World as a helper or ally, you can also gaze upon it and ask it directly to share with you what you might need now to ignite the process and stay the course. This card brings with it multiple indicators that you are destined for something bigger than you may have considered possible.

Journal Prompt

Write down anything that popped into your mind or vision during the meditation. Don't edit what you write; allow it to flow and don't leave out any details. Impressions can come spontaneously, and sometimes they only make more sense later.

CHAPTER TWELVE

The Minor Arcana

The minor arcana ("little secret") includes the four numbered suits: Wands, Swords, Pentacles, Cups, as well as court cards. I consider this portion of the tarot deck the cards that fill in the story. Reading the tarot is often like constructing the plot of a novel or screenplay. When you draw major arcana cards, they can be treated as the main characters, with its archetypes and mythological figures acting as protagonists or antagonists, significantly affecting the situation. The plotline or story arc is supplemented with the minor arcana, which fill in the circumstances, give a backdrop to the action, and reveal more of the internal psychological orientation to what is happening.

When only minor arcana appear in a reading, I encourage readers to revisit the same question again in a few days or a week to check in to see if something has changed. The minor arcana are highly fluid cards that disclose when we are dealing with something that is not truly set in stone or highly changeable and may require an open-minded attitude and willingness to be flexible. Life circumstances can change on a daily basis. Recognize when you need to release attachment and expectation to outcomes when working with the minor arcana.

In chapter two, we discussed the numbers in the tarot deck and the numerological significance of each card number. One meditation/study practice for learning the minor arcana is to memorize the element and number/meaning that corresponds with each suit. Filling in your readings with the card story is enriched by first realizing the other components as well. Each element has a significance that layers in meaning.

For review, the suits are as follows:

Wands = fire element = action and creativity
Swords = air element = mental activity, communication and decisions
Pentacles = earth element = money and values
Cups = water element = emotion and intuition

Minor Arcana Meditation Exercise

This meditation exercise uses only the minor arcana and is great for expanding your knowledge of the cards. One of the best ways to get more comfortable reading tarot cards is to study the patterns of the deck and the suits in particular through steady contemplation. First, organize the minor arcana by suit from Ace to 10 in each. Lay out each suit in rows on top of one another. Notice the similarities from suit to suit in the cards' story arc. Aces all showcase new beginnings in each suit but the meaning alters when we factor in the suit. Look at how the aces compare and contrast from suit to suit. The Ace of Pentacles differs from the Ace of Swords because Pentacles are represented by the earth element as well as money and values. Swords are related to the element of air and symbolize communication and decision making. New beginnings with communication (Swords) are different from new beginnings with money related matters (Pentacles). This type of active comparison helps you begin to build in layers of knowledge and add depth to your own readings.

Breathe, clear your mind, center yourself, ground your energy, and relax into this exercise.

Allow your gaze to fall on each numbered row. As you take in the images, connect your own life with these particular cards. Try not to control what pops into your mind; be open to the flow of thoughts, impressions, and information. If you sense or feel things stirring inside, take note of it. The images may surface memories from the past or inspire particular personal associations. Pay attention to how the cards help you tell your own life story when absorbed much like images from a graphic novel. This is a meditation exercise that can be done repeatedly. Each time you connect with the minor arcana in this way, you gain new perspectives based on where you are in your life path.

Getting to Know the Court Cards

While similar in nature to the major arcana's archetypes and mythological figures, in more practical terms the court cards represent actual people in our lives who are influencing the situation in question. They can also indicate aspects of our own psyche that may be surfacing. One of the best meditation and study methods for the court cards is to lay them all out in rows by suit and in order: Page, Knight, Queen, and King, four in each suit and sixteen total. Not only is this exercise a wonderful way to meditate, it also helps you memorize and remember these cards the next time they enter a reading.

Relax your mind and consider who in your life represents the cards before you, one at a time, and don't forget to include yourself in this character study. Who are the pages, knights, queens, and kings in your life? Take your time with this and have fun! My middle child is the Knight of Cups—sensitive and incredibly intuitive, often impulsive, acting only on gut feelings. She is also an activist and a risk taker, qualities I deeply admire. My oldest child would be the King of Wands. Like the powerful nobleman, he is a natural leader who is also highly social and was born under the zodiac sign Leo (fire sign). Wands in the tarot are represented by fire, so this is the perfect card for him. He is entrepreneurial in spirit, something else this card represents.

Paying attention to repetitive patterns in readings that include the minor arcana helps to more easily grasp the messages and wisdom they have to offer. I particularly encourage noticing repetitive number sequences and repetitive suits in a tarot reading. Repetitive number sequences can tell us where we are on the path to resolution of the issue in question. For example, if I have drawn more than one five of the suits, it is telling me I am at the situation's crisis or critical turning point, and something is likely to shift soon to move me beyond its intensity. Multiple cards drawn in one particular suit can indicate which area of life the question is affecting. For example, if I've drawn more than one Cups card, I know to probe deeper into how the situation is affecting me emotionally. Drawing more than one Wand card may be a clear message to take action or tap into my creativity.

I personally enjoy the highly changeable nature of the minor arcana cards. It feels empowering to reflect methodically on what I'm going through at any given moment, knowing that the cards will always be there to help me sort through my own internal processes as I go through each situation in my life. Pausing to absorb the wisdom in the cards assists me with navigating life circumstances with a calm, centered attitude.

CHAPTER THIRTEEN

Meditation
and the Wands

If your zodiac (Sun) sign is a fire sign (Aries, Leo, or Sagittarius), you may particularly connect with the energy of the wands suit. The wands in tarot symbolize the fire element, which is associated with determination, willpower, action, ambition, and creativity. The fire element can greatly humble us, as its force can both restore and destroy. It can cook and feed us, just as it can also take away what is most dear to us. This element is at play when we are our most passionate, energetic selves. I burn candles and light a fire in my hearth when I wish to connect with fire's motivating and catalyzing force.

At their best, the wands cards indicate where we are directing our efforts to improve our life circumstances. They can give us limitless amounts of energy and ignite our inner will to end any procrastinating tendencies and also show us when to engage our creativity. We may be taking a new step without knowing the outcome but know that it's time to stop stalling (Ace of Wands). The Three and Four of Wands show us the benefits of including others, asking for help, and feeling a deep sense of belonging. The conflict of the Five of Wands gives way to the joys of being triumphant and victorious with the Six of Wands. The hesitancy in action and need for structured activity and prioritization apparent in the Seven and Nine of Wands restores a sense of consistency and predictability of outcomes with the Eight of Wands. At their worst, the wands can exhibit areas where we are moving too quickly, our determination enforcing poor behavioral habits or workaholic tendencies. These attitudes can cause us to neglect other aspects of life (Ten of Wands). Wands may also surface when we are portraying our most temperamental, volatile, or reckless behaviors. Part of developing your own practice of the tarot includes learning about how we are handling the circumstances of our lives and empowering us to make different choices. If you have fire signs in your life, you know this energy quite well; if you are a fire sign yourself, you can deeply relate. Fire is often marked with a signature intensity that is palpable. When the fire sign closest to you is adamantly proving their point or dramatically and animatedly sharing a story, this is how the element manifests itself. It ignites the desire to take action. The wands tarot suit can show us where we have tended to things responsibly, or where we are falling short. There is no other suit that explicitly showcases our efforts besides the wands. The fire element is directly connected to the sun, the sustainer of all life. Honor the sacred in the fire element. Lean into fire when you need it to instigate action or ignite your own powers of will. Feel it surge through you by sending prayers to the direction of east at sunrise.

Respecting the potential for destruction is important if you intend to work with the Wands. They can inform us of our capacity to harness the more intense end of the emotional spectrum such as frustration and anger. Fire reminds us that controlled and calculated action rather than wild unchecked rage brings about the best results. We can use the energy of fire for creative pursuits as well, so use these cards as your muses. Reflect on them and channel the surges of energy pouring through you toward your own creative endeavors.

The wands connect us with the psychic skill of claircognizance, our own "inner knowing." This is where our strong and lightning-fast powers of perception can inspire action and motivate our inner will. We are moved by the passion-building strength of fire. Imagine in a moment of silence connecting to the fire in your own belly, that light that strikes sometimes when you least expect it and moves you to action. Use the wands in your tarot deck to further stimulate your sense of internal motivation through study and meditation.

Get Acquainted

Here is a way to meditate with the wands and get better acquainted with the fire element. First, lay out the cards in the wands suit face up in order from Ace to 10. Selecting the cards you most resonate with to understand what motivates you. Notice which card or cards are energizing you, and sink deeper into their wisdom to discern what action is being suggested of you. Sacred practices from many esoteric traditions have made use of the fire element for centuries. It is said that fire's energy purifies; building a fire and releasing intentions, prayers, or thoughts written onto paper is one way to send out intentions up to the universe. Remove the wands cards from the tarot deck. Shuffle or rifle through the cards and ask, "What inspired action serves me at this moment?" When ready, draw one card. Meditate on what area of life the card is indicating, and write down one thing you can do to shift that area of life for the better.

Wands Meditation

You may choose to light a candle or create a bonfire to meditate with the fire element. Candle gazing is an old school meditation technique with many benefits including improved focus, concentration, and spiritual wellness. It can have positive benefits for your inner vision and intuition as well. All candle gazing requires is fixating your gaze on a candle or several candles. If you'd rather not include actual fire in your meditation, you can generate a connection to the wands and fire element on your inner vision. Use the following imagery to connect with and ignite the wands from within.

With your eyes either open or closed, imagine a fire with your inner vision. If you don't see things in your mind's eye, use your own inner knowing to light this fire inside. Feel its warmth and energy penetrating your body. Try turning up the flame hotter and higher. Notice how this feels. Adjust the level of the fire to your own comfort. Feel the energy of this flame invigorating every single cell of your body.

Bring a life goal or a passion to mind. Allow the flicker of this flame to ignite your passion, and direct your focused attention toward your goal. Imagine what obstacles may cross your path in direct relation to this goal or passion. Feel your inner fire strengthening your resolve to overcome any and all obstacles. This intense element's strength helps you surface your own inner courage. You get to control your own inner fire—let it burn as hot and bright as you wish.

Now open your eyes and shuffle the wands again. Lay one card as guidance on how you may continue to connect with the energy of this element for good in your life.

Journal prompt: How did it feel to increase the flame inside? What lessons did the fire teach you? What message did your final wands card offer you for continuing to use this element and suit in your life?

CHAPTER FOURTEEN

Meditation and the Swords

If your zodiac (Sun) sign is an air sign: Gemini, Libra, or Aquarius, you may particularly connect more strongly with the energy of the swords suit. The swords in tarot symbolize the air element, which represents all aspects of the mind: thinking, ideas, decision, problem solving, and communication. At their best, the swords show us when we are thinking clearly, communicating well, and using the power of our own mind for positive decision making. At their worst, they show us when we are over-analyzing situations, being too harsh with others, making inappropriate decisions, or worrying to the detriment of our own mental well-being. This suit enriches questions requiring emotional detachment.

The swords can help us better gauge how to best navigate our own thought processes in the moment. I can't think of a better symbol for the mind than swords, as we know our thoughts have the tremendous capacity to cut or slice through and pierce any situation for positive or negative. As we wander through this suit, we can see moments of indecision, for example in the Two and Three of Swords. When we are called into mental rest with the Four or Six of Swords, we are given permission to release unhelpful or toxic patterns of thought. The Five or Seven of Swords may disclose when it is best to end any and all communication, conflict, or to relinquish the need for active problem solving. The Eight, Nine, and Ten of Swords show us where we may be over-analyzing, over-communicating, or spinning in our own thoughts. When those cards are drawn in a tarot reading, I advise activities that can help you safely process your thoughts in a healthy way through journaling, meditation, or, in more drastic situations, with a professional therapist.

The old adage that our thoughts are often our own worst enemies rings true with several of the cards in this suit. We can use the swords suit to better understand the goings on in our mind and thoughts from day to day. One of the most humbling reminders is the recognition that air both gives us life but takes it away from us in its absence. Meditation is the perfect pairing for working with the swords, as each breath we take connects us to the air element and opens us up to our own soul, bringing balance to our minds and hearts.

The swords suit connects us to our inner voice and our own clairaudience, or "clear hearing" psychic skill. Listening is an important passive action. When we master the art of listening to guidance from beyond, we can feel a consistent sense of connection to the invisible forces for good all around us. Messages are everywhere.

Reflect on the swords suit as a reminder to be open to the wisdom from the divine. Use them as a sort of key to open to your own inner voice. What's trying to come through you can further be understood with the help of the swords' mind stimulating magic.

Get Acquainted

Here are ways to meditate with the swords and get better acquainted with the air element and the suit of swords. First, lay out the cards in the swords suit in order from Ace to 10. Ponder the ways in which each card reminds you of a time in your life when you had to make a decision, or were stuck or confused about a particular life situation. Next, find a place in nature to sit. With your eyes closed, just breathe in through your nose and out through your mouth. Spend the next ten to fifteen minutes just noticing how the breeze or lack thereof feels on your skin and where it's coming from. Observe the clouds rolling by overhead and the birds flying around you, and marvel at the ways in which air supports us and our planet. Say a prayer of gratitude.

Shuffle or rifle the cards and ask the question "what do I need to know about my mind right now?" When ready, draw one card. What wisdom is it sharing with you about the inner workings of your mind? How might you use this knowledge to alter your thought processes?

Swords Meditation

Prepare for this meditation by finding a place inside or outside where you can sit or stand in a comfortable position with your eyes open and concentrate on your breath. Air is constantly circulating throughout our bodies. This meditation will remind us of the power of the air element and our ability to connect with it to heal. Sit or stand in a comfortable position with a lowered gaze and concentrate on your breath.

With each breath in, feel the air enter your nose and fill your lungs completely. Imagine the energy of air traveling to every single cell, tissue, organ of your body. As you breathe in, extend your spine and open your arms and chest space creating space for air. As you exhale, bring your hands together palm to palm and draw them to the center of your chest at your heart in a pose of gratitude. Acknowledge the importance of this element for survival. Follow each inhale and exhale and focus your intentions on the air, bringing deep healing and renewal to every nook and cranny of your mind, heart, body, and soul.

Complete your meditation by bringing your breathing back to a more normal pace and rhythm. Now gather the swords suit from your tarot deck and shuffle. Draw one card for guidance about how this suit can best serve and work with you. What does this card make you think about? What hidden thoughts or concerns does this card reveal to you now?

Journal prompt: How did it feel to connect with your breath? Did anything shift in your mind as you felt the energy of the air element circulating throughout your whole body?

CHAPTER FIFTEEN

Meditation
and the Pentacles

If your zodiac (Sun) sign is an earth sign (Taurus, Virgo, or Capricorn), you may particularly connect with the energy of the pentacles suit. The pentacles in tarot symbolize the earth element, which connects us to our material reality and our values: our bank accounts, investments, properties, the stuff we own, and what we consider our important things. The pentacles are also representative of the seeds we plant in life and the growth and abundance all around us. When our sense of security is infringed upon or our sense of stability wavers, the pentacles cards are likely to surface in a reading. In addition, see the pentacles cards in a reading when there is opportunity for entrepreneurship (Ace of Pentacles), changes to how we earn income (Two of Pentacles), when it is time to be more frugal and financially responsible (Four of Pentacles), showing the efforts for our hard work (Seven of Pentacles), or reaping what we have sown (Ten of Pentacles). At their best, they show us what we need to grow and sustain the life giving forces throughout our lives. At its worst, the earth element can overwhelm our ego and consume us with greedy, selfish, or miserly attitudes. The pentacles can also show us any overprotective or controlling ways.

The pleasures of the senses and maintaining a generous heart are ways in which we positively manifest the pentacles' gifts.

I often frame the pentacles cards as the farmers of the tarot deck. They show us where we have tended to things responsibly. Disciplined and diligent efforts are often required for something to grow. If we are on track or falling short, the pentacles will tell us what's needed to stay the course (Eight of Pentacles) or to turn a corner and get back on track (Five of Pentacles). Because this suit reveals to us our own vitality or ability to overcome physical adversity, we can also connect through the pentacles to understand health-related issues. Unlike the air element's intangible quality, the earth element is completely the opposite, dealing with the tangible things of life: what we touch, taste, own, and consume, centering more of life's sensual aspects.

The earth element is formed as a combination of the work of the air, water, and fire. We are greatly humbled in our awareness of our complete and utter dependency as a species on the earth for sustenance. We are able to channel the messages the earth is here to provide us because nature is constantly relating to us, collaborating in this great wheel of life within which we are all connected. We come from the earth, and our bodies return to it at death. We cannot live without the abundance the earth provides for us. We would also do well to heed its warnings when it is in pain and suffering, which it is as a result of climate change. We cannot deny the importance of the tremendous care we each need to take to ensure its survival. It is beautiful to honor the gifts it offers us through sacred practices such as meditation.

The pentacles can help us handle the responsibilities of life, our material resources, money-related matters, and health concerns. This suit can also help us build in a more conscious awareness of mother earth's gifts. Draw upon these cards for reflective guidance when feelings of instability surface. I see the pentacles often come up during card readings related to job or career path changes, questions about how to best harness financial resources, changes with home location, buying or selling homes, and whenever personal values are coming into question. Our values shift as we age, and the pentacles can help us realize this and make adjustments to our life goals.

The pentacles and earth element connect us with the psychic skill of clairvoyance, or our own "inner seeing." The pentacles assist us in grounding ourselves and opening to our own inner vision. Imagine the spinning disc that is your own third eye rotating and opening as you gaze upon the cards.

Get Acquainted

Here are some ways to meditate with the pentacles and get better acquainted with the earth element. First, lay out the cards in the earth suit in order from Ace to 10. Which cards inspire you to take action for greater stability and security? Notice which card or cards feel like a good fit for where you currently are in your life and why they are an accurate representation. Next, connect with the healing energies of the earth through a technique called earthing. Walk barefoot in a park, hug a tree, plant something, create an altar made of crystals and stones in your yard, rest in the shade of a tree with your bare hands touching the ground, or connect heart to heart with mother earth, laying belly down on the ground. Be quiet and sense or feel mother earth's heartbeat. Send thoughts of love and healing down into the ground. Finally, remove the pentacles cards from your tarot deck. Shuffle or rifle the cards and ask the question "what do I need to feel more stable and secure right now?" When ready, draw one card. What is one action step you can you take based on the card drawn?

Pentacles Meditation

Connect with the pentacles and earth element in this brief yet powerful meditation. This is a simple grounding exercise to bring you fully into your body and heighten your awareness of your own connection with the earth. Sit or stand with your feet on the ground and take a moment to express gratitude to the planet that feeds us and sustains all of life. Imagine golden cords of light connected at each of the soles of your feet, and feel the energy of those cords of energy flowing down and connecting with the earth's core, where healing is abundant and all of life originates and is created. Feel how good it is to be truly connected, tethered, and grounded to the earth. Feel the renewal of your own energy giving back directly to the heart of the earth.

Sense the energy of the earth's core rising up to meet you now as the spiral of healing energy enters through the soles of your feet. Feel the energy cycle up now through your legs, hips, belly, and torso, permeating every cell, organ, and tissue, coursing out the top of your head to connect you with the Divine. Grounding not only merges us with the healing superpowers of the planet, it also helps us create a bridge with the universe's spiritual forces.

Now shuffle the pentacles suit in your tarot deck and draw one card. How does this card inform you about what area of life to ground yourself in now? In more practical terms, notice where it advises more attentiveness with your own personal finances, bank accounts, values, or health concerns.

Journal prompt: What did it feel like to ground your energy and merge with the earth's core? Make a list of simple ways you can include grounding and connecting with the Earth's energy for a greater sense of stability and security.

CHAPTER SIXTEEN

Meditation and the Cups

If your zodiac (Sun) sign is a water sign (Cancer, Scorpio, or Pisces), you may particularly connect with the energy of the cups suit. The cups in tarot symbolize the water element, which connects us to our emotions, imagination, and intuition. It best resembles our inner landscape and can be incredibly helpful when trying to sort through emotional confusion. I use the suit of cups for my own personal shadow work, or the practice of intentionally addressing subconscious fears, old emotional wounds, and areas of trauma in the effort to relinquish the hold the past has on us. As we are human beings, we are served by honoring that we have a dark as well as a light side. Sometimes through dealing with unresolved grief or loss, we can touch base with our shadow, which is just as important as work that brings us to the light. I cherish the cups of the tarot, especially when I need a little nudge because I'm confused about how I'm actually feeling and why. The cups are a support network of sorts, lending comfort and understanding. When I'm down or low, seeing the Four of Cups in a tarot spread reminds me that moments of emotional upset are fleeting and also a natural part of life. If I'm in a celebratory mood, the Three or Ten of Cups may encourage celebration, social activity, or connection outside of ourselves. The wisdom of the Five and Eight of Cups directs me to look toward the future and work hard to put the past behind me. The Six and Seven of Cups lend an inspired vibe of possibility and the inspiration to choose what brings me the most joy. If you are someone who identifies as sensitive or empathic, know that the cups can become a source of comfort and nurturing, not to mention a way to grow your own emotional strength and resiliency.

When drawn, the cups can indicate whether we are grounded in reality or fantasy at any given moment. The cups suit shows us where we have tended our emotional health with due diligence as well as where we have neglected and buried old wounds. They can show us where we are overreacting to something or under-reacting through avoidance or denial. The cups can motivate us to deal with emotional pain and trauma directly and represent our capacity to invite healing processes. The Two of Cups specifically encourages healing in relationships but also can indicate a need for healthy boundaries so a relationship can grow and flourish. I find the Nine and Ten of Cups to be two of the most peaceful and comforting cards in the entire deck. However, it is important to maintain a sense of humility, especially to avoid a boastful or arrogant attitude about our good fortune.

All of the elements support and sustain life but can just as easily remove and destroy it. Water is the giver of life as well as its sustainer—we grow in a watery womb for nine months. However, it also has a destructive side, evident in the uncontrollable nature of flooding. Ocean waves are exciting to watch, play in, and surf on, but they can be dangerous if not respected. In all its fury, water is impossible to control and can take out everything in its path. Waves of emotion can wash over us; when we can safely navigate them, they can help us to better understand ourselves. However, when we lack the tools to deal with strong emotions, they can wreak havoc on our relationships and surroundings. Addressing and healing emotional trauma is an ongoing process that feeds us throughout our lives.

The cups connect us with the psychic skill of clairsentience, or our "clear feeling." Whether we wish to better understand our emotions or sharpen our intuition, the cups cards create an avenue of internal exploration. They can assist in heightening our senses and opening our sixth sense to any intuitive stirrings. The cups support our heart's growth and healing. They affirm that we are fully capable of connecting to the undercurrents of emotional connection and intimacy in our relationships while fostering empathy for the world around us.

Get Acquainted

You can meditate with the cups and get better acquainted with the water element. First, lay out the cards in the cups suit in order from Ace to 10. Choose a few cups cards that seem to resonate with how you are feeling emotionally at the moment. Reflect for a moment on why the stories in those cards may be a good fit. Next, immerse yourself in water, one of the strongest ways to connect with this element. Sit in a hot tub and watch the steam float up around you. Breathe and observe the magical quality of the different forms water can transform into. Ponder within yourself how emotion acts as a compass that guides you and helps you understand what you need at any given moment. If you can't sit in a tub, walk by a river, stream, or ocean. You can also use an app or YouTube that allows you to listen to the waves of the ocean or the falling rain. Even just listening can connect you with the element of water as strongly as being near or in it. Place your hand on your heart and breathe into your heart space, noticing where your feelings are. Finally, shuffle or rifle the cups cards and ask, "What do

I need to grow emotional resiliency?," or "How can I best use my emotions to inform and guide me?" When ready, draw one card. What do you feel the card is offering you for guidance?

Cups Meditation

Use this meditation to connect with the energy of the water element. While it is handy to sit near a source of water such as a pond, fountain, river, lake, or ocean, it is absolutely not necessary. You can play a video on YouTube of the sound of ocean waves or falling rain. You can also simply meet with the water element in your own inner vision.

First, tend to your breath. Sit, lay down, or stand somewhere comfortable for you. Allow the energy of your breath to wash over you. Close your eyes and imagine your breath bringing gentle ocean waves of cleansing and healing over your whole body. See, sense, or feel the energy of your heart opening now, as you move those waves through your back and out the front of your chest now.

Keep your breath engaged, smooth, rhythmic, and flowing like the movement of a stream or river. Keep this motion continuous for several minutes, noticing the similarities between air and water, their flexibility, and yet at the same time their relentlessness. Water goes where it wishes to go, whether we control it or not. Face any fears you may have of this powerful element's exacting potential. Digging deep now, find your courage, and feel yourself surrendering to the positive healing powers of this beautiful ally and helper.

Sense areas in your body where you may have stuck or trapped emotion lingering. Breathe into those areas of your body, releasing emotional residue. Feel the water element flowing throughout your body, and sense or see this energy coursing through your veins, providing restoration and nourishment to your blood flowing out to every extremity.

Give yourself a few moments in silence to just breathe. Continue to see and feel the revitalizing energy of the water element as it flows through you. Surrender to this flow and accept its gifts. Notice it now washing away from your body, heart, and mind any stagnant energy that no longer serves you. Notice yourself feeling cleansed of this energy as your shoulders relax, your heart feeling more peaceful.

Shuffle the cups suit in your tarot deck and pull one card. Study and reflect on how this card is informing you of your own inner emotional landscape, depth, growth, and capacity for loving. Journal prompt: What emotions surfaced during this meditation? How did it feel to get out of your mind and into your heart? How can you use the cups cards for further emotional healing and self-awareness?

CHAPTER SEVENTEEN

Meditation and the Court Cards

While similar to the archetypes in the major arcana, the court cards are different in their symbolism. During a tarot reading, they often divulge who in our own lives might be affecting or influencing the situation in question. If not referring to others in our lives, they can also represent qualities of our own personalities or our skills and talents we may draw upon.

When I began reading tarot for myself and others, I really struggled with the court cards; I found the images distracting and unrelatable due to the tone of nobility embedded in each of them. I found it difficult to make a practical connection to the question or current situation until I laid them all out and began studying them as actual people or "characters" from my own life. The meditations in this chapter can assist you in opening the door to a profound link of understanding to who these figures are in the plot of your own life story.

You will gain a tremendous amount of power over your deck when you learn to commit to memory certain associations with the individual cards and suits as a whole. The meditation exercises here are designed to help you get close to the characters so they will be more recognizable to you in future readings.

Mini Court Card Meditation

Separate out the court cards from your tarot deck: the pages, knights, queens, and kings. Organize them by suit in rows stacked to make columns of the same court member.

With all the court cards laid out before you now, study the columns of pages, knights, queens, and kings slowly and methodically, one at a time. Allow a person you associate with each card to enter your mind. More specifically, what characteristics about the character in the card do you associate with that particular person in your life? For example, if you have super sensitive and intuitive people in your life, check out the cups court cards for assignment. These are the people you know who have tender hearts and are in tune with their emotions. They could also be the therapists or spiritual healers in your life. The intellectuals and deep thinkers, talkers, and conversationalists may be at home in the swords court cards. These are the folks who love information and work with words. They're big on communication, have opinions, and love to feel heard and listened to. The busy-bodied, energetic, active go-getters in your life can be assigned to the wands. They are the people you know who don't like to sit down or whom you find to be warm, inspirational, and creative. Be sure to assign one or more of the court cards to yourself! It's helpful to journal your study and findings for future reference.

The next step is to meditate with each of the court characters and make them personal. For instance, pages represent our inner youthful self. Reflect on what you can do to engage your own inner child. Allow your own playful spirit to emerge. Notice what your intuition and imagination is revealing to you about engaging your inner playful self. Pages also represent messengers between worlds, here to bring you important mystical or esoteric information from other realms. As you grow more mesmerized by the images in the pages, invite these youthful messengers to channel any communication from other realms. Choose the one that feels the most resonant for this moment and activate their energy within you.

The knights are similar to the Fool from the major arcana; they represent active energy, motivation, risk, and impulsiveness. They inspire us to take action and follow through with unfinished business. They can move through us rather spontaneously, and we are typically unprepared to meet their energy. With the knights before you now, reflect on where in your life you might employ a bit of their impulsive, active energy. Choose the knight card, suit, and element that best supports the life situation coming to your mind. Write down a possible course of action you may take. With the knights, it is best to take a moment to do a bit of reality testing before moving forward, as they can tend to inspire a bit of recklessness in their darkest hour.

The queens connect with the social, emotional, and spiritual aspects of our lives. They promote gentleness, receptivity, and connection. The queens are often associated with mother energy; the kings representing father energy. With the queens before you now, reflect on where in your life you give in nurturing ways to guide, support, and comfort others. Bring a situation to mind where you felt more compassion and care was needed. Choose the queen card that best represents the characteristics and demeanor you can access to support you now.

The kings represent the epitome of personal power. They show us where we are accessing our own ability to be assertive, decisive, and to take the lead. They can be seen as the parts of you that automatically know how to handle whatever obstacle may come your way with clarity and action. With the kings before you, bring to mind a situation in your life in which you may feel dis-empowered. Identify specific challenges you face. Choose the king that best represents the qualities you will need to overcome this situation. You can enter the story in this card and ask the king for further wisdom to proceed.

Court Card Meditation

This meditation is not necessarily specific to the court cards, but it's easiest to start with them because they are the easiest to visualize due to their concrete imagery. Choose ritual tools to supplement this visualization meditation. Perhaps you would like to gather a crystal such as amethyst (increases psychic awareness) or do a little smoke clearing to prepare the space. Take your time and be sure you won't be disturbed. The meditation won't take more than ten to fifteen minutes.

Now shuffle the court cards well and draw one. Sit or lie down comfortably. If you're lying down, it may be best to place the card over either your heart or your third eye to enhance your connection to its energy. Close your eyes and hold the court card image in your mind's eye. See, sense, or feel them reaching out to you, inviting you to take a journey with them. A corridor appears before you now or perhaps a long, winding road through the woods or by a stream. Choose one that is most appealing to you.

Walk with the figure in the card. You can ask them questions if you'd like or just listen to see if they have anything to say. What are they showing you? Spend time with them observing. Bring all of your senses to the fore now, smelling, seeing, hearing, feeling, and tasting what there is to experience. The more real you make this in your inner vision, the more you'll gain from it. When it feels right, thank them for their guidance. Breathe, allow the images to dissipate, and slowly come back into your body.

Journal prompt: Write yourself any messages that the court card figure had for you. What was it like to join the story of this card and meet a new friend?

Conclusion

This book has laid out a comprehensive method for working with your tarot deck in tandem with meditation. When you set the mood with lighting, music, and sacred objects, you establish a regular predictable rhythm that all your senses including your sixth sense can easily engage with. Creating your own sacred rituals to support your meditation and tarot practice lends such a magical and special quality to an everyday spiritual tool. Incorporating the meditation techniques that you love here will only enhance your tarot practice. My hope is that your curiosity was ignited and these pages gave you sufficient foundational tools to work with. It's the sort of book that you can earmark favorite exercises and chapters; you don't need to read it through every time. Give yourself the opportunity to experiment with all the various meditation techniques in this book, and I know you will narrow down your favorites. Not everyone works the same, so lend yourself a bit of grace as you navigate the wide variety of exercises and information present here.

Unlocking the gateway to self-awareness through tarot and meditation will serve you for the rest of your life. Tarot is a lifelong practice and tool. Reaching mastery requires diligence, patience, as well as lots of exploration and time. You will inevitably surprise yourself when you begin to unleash your own inner wisdom and connection through the techniques shared in these pages.

One of the greatest tarot experts and creators, Rachel Pollack, crossed over April 7, 2023, leaving behind an indelible body of work. I offer a small tribute to her here, as I know within the greater tarot community her direct influence and mentorship will be dearly missed. Luckily, we have many of her gems of wisdom available to us. If you don't already own it, consider adding her 1988 work, *Seventy-Eight Degrees of Wisdom* to your library. Rachel was known as perhaps the first tarot authority to look at the tarot from a psychological and subconscious framework rather than simply from an esoteric or symbolic one. Being able to understand the self, how we tick, our mind's inner workings, and what might be hidden from view is a sophisticated and healing way to engage with tarot's wisdom. I truly believe this perspective is why the tarot has flourished for the decades since Rachel first shared her philosophies with us. She opened us up to going beyond using tarot as a "fortune telling" tool.

In her 1999 book, *Haindl Tarot: The Major Arcana*, Rachel wrote:

> Used correctly, Tarot cards increase free will. The more information we can gather about ourselves and our situations, the more we can make wise choices. In fact, the action of consulting the Tarot changes the very situation that the cards are describing. The person knows more than before. If we gain greater awareness and personal power from Tarot readings, we can learn other things as

well. First of all, we learn about the cards themselves. The more we use them, the more we understand their meanings and subtleties. Some people believe they must study each card and memorize all its symbolism before they dare to do a reading. But if we start using them, we not only accelerate the learning process, we also discover new ideas not found in any of the books.

Tarot readings teach us about human nature not just with the lessons in the cards but also from the people themselves, including their questions and in their reactions to what a reading is telling them.[1]

When we pair our tarot practice with meditation, we offer ourselves the chance to move beyond rote memorization of the cards. Making a more intimate internal connection with the cards brings us into a deeply receptive space for understanding the self. Tarot animates our own inner workings, while meditation techniques open an avenue of deeper concentration, insight, and awareness. When our mind is calm, the images and stories can come to life and work through us, revealing exactly where we are emotionally or psychologically in the moment. Subconscious patterning or conditioning we are striving to release and heal can more easily surface when we are in a neutral receptive atmosphere. Tarot and meditation fit together beautifully, and once you begin merging the two disciplines, you'll find a wealth of insight and self-awareness available to you.

There is a never-ending wealth of tarot knowledge to be gained once we grasp the basics and establish a personal connection with the cards. In the next section is a list of my most cherished

---

1   Rachel Pollack, *Haindl Tarot: The Major Arcana* (Newburyport, MA: New Page Books, 1999), 182–183.

meditation and tarot resources that I hope helps you add to what this book has to offer. Don't be afraid to mix up your tarot and meditation practice, and try out different philosophies, techniques, and ideas.

Recommended Reading

Meditation

Alasia, Silvana. *Color Meditation Cards*. Woodbury, MN: Llewellyn Worldwide, 2023.

Bodri, William. *The Little Book of Meditation: The Way to Lifelong Vibrant Health, Peace of Mind, Spiritual Growth and Wellbeing*. Reno, NV: Top Shape Publishing, LLC, 2011.

Chödrön, Pema. *How to Meditate: A Practical Guide to Making Friends with Your Mind*. Louisville, CO: Sounds True, 2013.

Erickson, Lisa. *The Art and Science of Meditation: How to Deepen and Personalize Your Practice*. Woodbury, MN: Llewellyn Worldwide, 2020.

Hanh, Thich Nhat. *The Miracle of Mindfulness: An Introduction to the Practice of Meditation*. Boston: Beacon Press, 1999.

Hay, Louise L., and Jill Kramer. *Meditations to Heal Your Life*. Carlsbad, CA: Hay House, 2000.

Mager, Stefan. *Meditation Guide*. Woodbury, MN: Llewellyn Worldwide, 2023.

Tubali, Shai. *Llewellyn's Complete Book of Meditation: A Comprehensive Guide to Effective Techniques for Calming Your Mind and Spirit*. Woodbury, MN: Llewellyn Worldwide, 2023.

Tarot

Adam, Elliot. *The Fearless Tarot: How to Give a Positive Reading in Any Situation*. Woodbury, MN: Llewellyn Worldwide, 2020.

Bartlett, Sarah. *The Tarot Bible*. New York: Sterling, 2006.

Blake, Deborah, and Elisabeth Alba. *Everyday Witch Tarot*. Woodbury, MN: Llewellyn Worldwide, 2017.

Bunning, Joan. *The Big Book of Tarot*. Newburyport, MA: Weiser, 2019.

Cynova, Melissa. *Kitchen Table Tarot: Pull Up a Chair, Shuffle the Cards, and Let's Talk Tarot*. Woodbury, MN: Llewellyn Worldwide, 2017.

Fiebig, Johannes, and Evelin Burger. *The Ultimate Guide to the Rider Waite Tarot*. Woodbury, MN: Llewellyn Worldwide, 2013.

Graham, Sasha, and Abigail Larson. *Dark Wood Tarot*. Woodbury, MN: Llewellyn Worldwide, 2020.

Greer, Mary K., and Tom Little. *Understanding the Tarot Court*. Woodbury, MN: Llewellyn Worldwide, 2004.

Katz, Marcus, and Tali Goodwin. *Around the Tarot in 78 Days: A Personal Journey Through the Cards*. Woodbury, MN: Llewellyn Worldwide, 2012.

Law, Stephanie Pui-Mun, and Barbara Moore. *Shadowscapes Tarot*. Woodbury, MN, Llewellyn Worldwide, 2010.

Michelsen, Teresa. *The Complete Tarot Reader: Everything You Need to Know from Start to Finish*. Woodbury, MN: Llewellyn Worldwide, 2022.

Moore, Barbara. *Tarot for Beginners: A Practical Guide to Reading the Cards*. Woodbury, MN: Llewellyn Worldwide, 2010.

———. *Your Tarot Your Way*. Woodbury, MN: Llewellyn Worldwide, 2016.

Place, Robert M. *The Tarot: History, Symbolism, and Divination*. New York: TarcherPerigree, 2005.

Pollack, Rachel. *Seventy-Eight Degrees of Wisdom: A Tarot Journey to Self-Awareness*. Newburyport, MA: Weiser, 2020.

———. *Haindl Tarot: The Major Arcana*. Newburyport, MA: New Page Books, 1999.

Reed, Theresa. *Tarot: No Questions Asked*. Newburyport, MA: Weiser, 2020.

Robertson, Leeza, and Julie Dillon. *Mermaid Tarot*. Woodbury, MN: Llewellyn Worldwide, 2019.

Rosengarten, Arthur. *Tarot and Psychology: Spectrums of Possibility*. St. Paul, MN: Paragon House, 2000.

Waite, Arthur Edward, and Pamela Colman Smith. *The Rider Tarot*. Stamford, CT: US Games, 1971.

To Write to the Author

If you wish to contact the author or would like more information about this book, please write to the author in care of Llewellyn Worldwide Ltd. and we will forward your request. Both the author and publisher appreciate hearing from you and learning of your enjoyment of this book and how it has helped you. Llewellyn Worldwide Ltd. cannot guarantee that every letter written to the author can be answered, but all will be forwarded. Please write to:

Chanda Parkinson
℅ Llewellyn Worldwide
2143 Wooddale Drive
Woodbury, MN 55125-2989

Please enclose a self-addressed stamped envelope for reply,
or $1.00 to cover costs. If outside the U.S.A., enclose
an international postal reply coupon.

Many of Llewellyn's authors have websites with additional information and resources. For more information, please visit our website at http://www.llewellyn.com.